STORYTELLING
BY THE
NUMBERS

JOHN BUCHER

www.sideshowmediagroup.com
8033 Sunset Blvd. #164
Los Angeles, CA. 90046

Many of the pieces included in this book first appeared at la-screenwriter.com. Special thanks to Angela Bourassa for her support and permission to use them here.

Published by Sideshow Media Group
8033 Sunset Blvd. #164
Los Angeles, CA. 90046
USA

sideshowmediagroup.com

CONTENTS

For my father, John K. Bucher, who showed me that being a writer was possible and now daily inspires me through his storytelling and commitment to his craft.

ONE INTERVIEW ABOUT HAMLET, *MAD MEN* AND UNIVERSALS IN STORYTELLING:

A TALK WITH ROBERT MCKEE

Robert McKee has become synonymous with the word *story*. He is the most sought after screenwriting lecturer in the world. A Fulbright scholar, his students have included over 60 Academy Award winners, 200 Academy Award nominees, and hundreds of Emmy and DGA winners. Peter Jackson has referred to him as "The Guru of Gurus." And, of course, Brian Cox's portrayal of him in the Oscar-nominated film, *Adaptation,* has become legendary. In this two-part interview, I discuss story's past, present, and future with the man who literally wrote the book on the subject – Robert McKee.

JOHN BUCHER: I'm often reminded of a quote from Flannery O'Connor, who said that everyone knows what a story is until they sit down to write one. What makes a good story? Is there such a thing as a bad story?

ROBERT MCKEE: Well, of course there are and we suffer through thousands every year, but the answer to the question what's a good story, what makes a good story, really depends on point of view. My definition of a good story, from the audience's point of view, is very simple. It hooks, holds and pays off.

It hooks their interest, emotionally and intellectually, and it holds their interest, and deepens their involvement emotionally, and increases their curiosity, intellectually, and then finally it pays off an experience that satisfies their expectations for both the head and the heart. It hooks. It holds. It pays off.

JOHN BUCHER: What would you say is universal in storytelling? Obviously you give your talks all over the world and the things you have to say connect with people from every country in the world. So, what is universal in storytelling and what is specific to cultures?

ROBERT MCKEE: Well, let's begin with what's universal. There's a whole set of fundamentals, like curiosity. You have to take an audience through time such that they are unaware of the passage of time. An hour, two, three hours go by and suddenly they're looking at their watch saying, "My god, it's over." You have to engage their curiosity so that they're constantly grabbing handfuls in the future looking ahead and do not notice the passage of time, that is a universal.

There must also be, at some level, conflict. It may or may not be surface. It may be inner-conflict. It may be very subdued and suppressed. It may be very overt. It may be on any level of life; physical, social, personal, inner, even subconscious, but somehow within the story, the struggle to achieve whatever it is the character needs is met with antagonism. They can't get what they want the easy way.

There must be a value at stake, at least one. It could be very complex. It could be many values, but there has to be a core value that is the essential subject matter of the story; justice, injustice, a meaningful life versus a meaningless life, love and hate, aloneness versus togetherness, immaturity, maturity, a lacking of humanity, a gaining of humanity or a loss of humanity, degeneration plot and so forth and so there has to be a value, and values come in as a binary, positive and negative.

The movement of a story everywhere in the world, universally, is a dynamic movement from positive to negative in terms of whatever value is at stake, building positive negative, positive negative and progressing in terms of the jeopardy or the risk that's at stake in the character's lives. And often where differences lie in terms of culture is in this issue of values.

For example, I lecture often in China, and Chinese culture is founded on respect for authority, and

indeed even further than that, obedience to authority.
And the father figure and the mother figure, but
particularly the father figure dominates culture and
characters, politicians or whoever, teachers and
so forth, people in authority are looked up to and
respected outwardly in least in terms of behavior.
In America, you remember back in the 60s or 70s,
there were bumper stickers that said, "question
authority." Here, we value independence. We value
rebellion against authority because in our culture,
authority has a negative connotation. And in politics
today, all our complaints about the inequities in the
economy, accusation of the rich abusing their money
to pull strings is a rebellion against authority. So, if
you make a film about rebellion against authority in
the United States, it may have great success. If you
make that same film in China, the censors may not
even allow it to be shown.

So, there are great differences from culture to culture
in terms of the perception of values. Some cultures,
for example, are very romantic. Love, romantic love
has got tremendous value. I read a study some time
ago when I was preparing my Love Story lecture, that
they went around the world asking this question, "Are
you, at the moment, in love?" They discovered that the
most romantic culture in the world is Russian. 75% of
all people in Russia believe that they are currently in

love. The least romantic culture tended to be Arabic
or Islamic cultures, where less than 50% believed that
they were currently in love. Our notion of romantic
love in American's is somewhere like around 60%.
And so our notion of romantic love is not the same as
the Russians. It's not the same as the Egyptians. They
all have romantic love, but the degree to which they
idolize it varies. Once you understand the core value
at the heart of the story and once the audience can
experience or understand that value, then the dynamic
is universal. This is why we can enjoy foreign films
-- films from very different cultures -- so long as the
filmmaker makes us understand what's at stake.

Another universal is empathy. You could have great
curiosity and that might hold you through the story,
but there's no suspense. Curiosity is not the same
thing as suspense. Suspense is emotional curiosity.
And so when the audience empathizes with the
protagonist, recognizes shared humanity, they say,
"she is a human being just like me." When they then
invest in the core character, and want that character
to have whatever the character wants, then they're
emotionally involved and then you have tremendous
suspense.

These things are true in every culture. How
exactly those things get used is different. Take

time for example. In Japanese culture they have an
enormously powerful patience, and they will accept a
much more static story than we Americans will. And
you could reach a certain point in the story in Japan
where the characters are in some sort of crisis, and
just cut to an image of Mount Fuji, and leave that
snow-capped mountain on the screen for two or three
minutes, and the Japanese will sit there thinking
about the problem the characters are facing, as they
look at this image. Americans say, "Why are we
cutting to the mountain?"

JOHN BUCHER: Can you speak a little bit about the
structural relationship between the protagonist and
the antagonist?

ROBERT MCKEE: Well, structurally, the protagonist
is one person, man, woman, child at the heart of the
story, but [there] could be co-protagonists, like *Thelma
and Louise*. You could have a trio, like *The Witches
of Eastwick*. You could have *The Dirty Dozen*. The
size of the protagonist, the number of people involved
varies from story to story, but when they all want the
same thing, they're all struggling toward that desire
and they suffer and benefit mutually, they're still just
"the protagonist," no matter how many there are. So,
protagonist varies in that way. The same thing can
be said about an antagonist. It could be, you know,

multiple antagonists in an action film. You have archvillians, you have all their goons, and assassins and femme fatales and the societies to be rescued and armies to be defeated, and so the size of an antagonist striking, again may be massive.

On the other hand, the protagonist can be his own worst enemy. Take for example that marvelous television series, *Mad Men*. Don Draper has any number of antagonists through his career -- his marriages and so forth, people who are opposed to what he wants, but he is the antagonist. His damaged childhood, his experience in Korea, and his attempt to lead somebody else's life, that has been eating away at him decade after decade, driving him into alcoholism and all the rest. He is the protagonist and antagonist of the story. And so structurally, the protagonist is one side we empathize with. The other side (antagonist) we don't.

In horror films you have victim protagonist and monster antagonist, but in many horror films, we get on the monster's side, and we actually identify with the monster to a point because we love their power, and power's a very attractive thing. We would really love to have the power of a monster at times. Just to settle scores. So you can't even say that the structure is that we always empathize with the protagonist and we're always opposed to the antagonist. It's not always the case. In certain stories we get on both sides. Sometimes the audience is switching sides back and forth, back and forth. In certain stories the antagonist is ubiquitous. With Samuel Beckett, the antagonist is time. Living in time and knowing that it's going to run out. So the antagonist doesn't even have a personality. It's just a condition of life and bringing about what we used to call the existential crisis. I mean a protagonist is simply the character whose life has gone out of bounds and they are struggling down the spine of action to restore the balance of life. All stories are essentially that. A protagonist's struggle to put life back on an even keel, somehow to restore the balance.

I know what people want. What your readers want is an easy, clear, concrete, straightforward statement: do this, and you will be successful. Don't do this, because you won't be successful. But, John, I'm going to give you answers that take in the whole of storytelling. So part of my teaching is just to make it clear to people that when you ask a question like what's a protagonist, what's an antagonist, there's no single answer to that question. And, therefore, you're going to have to use your imagination and think it through. There's no formula. There's just form.

JOHN BUCHER: What you're saying definitely feels more true than any formula anyone could approach. I'm definitely with you.

ROBERT MCKEE: That's good. I hope you can convince your readers of that, too, because in the panic to achieve, to try to make a living doing this, often people will resort to the most simplistic cliché answers to these questions, and just copy. They copy what other people do thinking, "Well, this is what made them successful, and I can do some little variation off of this and it will make me successful." But the great writers only concentrate on the relationship between them and their audience and they want to express their knowledge of life uniquely. They don't have to resort to difference for the sake of difference and a lot of bad filmmakers do. Look at long form television. We're witnessing some of the greatest writing ever in America. And these, these people who are writing these great series are not looking over their shoulder. They are out there exploring and doing things -- 100 hours of drama, doing things that no one has ever attempted before. The complexity of character in these great long form series is infinitely greater than anything that was ever done in film, ever. I do a TV day, a whole day study of what makes a great TV series, and the key is character, and complexity of character. Because, people will follow a TV series as long as the central character is changing, evolving in some way, or being revealed. I mean, there's secrets or there's aspects of this character that have been there since the beginning of the series and they are now being dramatized and brought out. So the character's either being revealed for who they've always been, but we didn't know, or they're evolving into a character we didn't know, but one way or another through revelation or change, the character is not staying the same. Once that character's exhausted, they cannot change, there's nothing left to reveal in them, the series is over. This is what happened with *Dexter*, for example. Two or three seasons before the end of the run, Dexter was exhausted and we just ran out of interest. On the other hand, in *Breaking Bad*, Walter White was still being revealed until the very last scene. We always suspected he cared for Jessie, but then he throws himself between Jessie and the bullets, he's still being revealed. In film, we talk about the three-dimensional character, which is a cliché. Usually characters are more dimensional than that, at least central characters are, but three is a sort of standard. I did a study of Tony Soprano as a 12 dimensional character, and I did a study of Walter White as a 16 dimensional character. They have 80, 100 hours of storytelling, and what brings out dimensions primarily is the relationship between characters. So when you have 100 hours of storytelling and you have a cast of

20-30 characters, every time the protagonist meets another character, it brings out a different quality in him, or the same character in another circumstance as the story evolves brings out another quality in him. And so they "dimensionalize" each other by the way in which they react with each other, because we don't react to different people [in] the same [way]. You don't treat the clerk at the 7-11 the way you treat the cop who pulls you over for a ticket. They're both strangers. The relationship is social but the power's not the same, so you don't treat one the way you treat the other. Understanding that then, you design the cast of characters, such that whenever two characters meet they bring out different sides of each other.

Hamlet used to be thought of as the most complex character ever written, and maybe he was or is through his time in the theatre, but he only has four hours. And he only has relationships with six or eight other people, and so in that four hours and in those relationships, his complexities are all revealed and he changes. But, that's only four hours and six people.

JOHN BUCHER: Hamlet, Tony Soprano, Walter White, all these guys in a sense are anti-heroes. Is it possible to develop a multi-dimensional character with a traditional hero or does the anti-hero just lend themselves more to multidimensionality?

ROBERT MCKEE: The answer's probably not. A hero is a character. I mean if we take the strict definition because people use the word hero for anything and it just means leading character. Most leading characters or core characters are not heroic, they're just struggling to get through their day with the best life has given them. A hero literally means somebody who willingly risks or even sacrifices their life for the lives of others. That's a hero.

If we go by that definition, Tom Cruise, in an action film, he's a hero. He will risk his life for other people, sacrifice it if necessary for them. That drive for justice, to save society, and risk or sacrifice your own life, doesn't leave much room for complication. So, the action hero is by definition pretty slender in terms of their dimensionality. The anti-hero that you're talking about would be characters like Walter White, Tony Soprano, and Don Draper. These are characters who have a clear dynamic between good and evil. They are good evil people, evil good people. They go back and forth between the positive and the negative in terms of morality. And these characters, they're mainly not anti-heroes in the traditional sense of anti-hero. The anti-hero is somebody Humphrey Bogart used to play. He had a private and personal code. The character of Mike, in *Breaking Bad* and now in *Better Call Saul*, is an anti-hero, because he has a personal code. He's a criminal. He'll kill people if necessary. But he keeps [loyal to] his gangster code [too].

It's like in *The Godfather*. They were loyal to the Godfather's family, and outside the family everything goes. Those are anti-heroes. Walter White is not such a character. Don Draper is not such a character. Walter finally does, in the long run, take care of his family and leave them some money. In the climax of Mad Men, when Don Draper's ex-wife gets lung cancer and he's got two young sons, at one point, he says, "I'll come back and I'll take care of my sons," and the ex-wife says, "No, I'm going to give them to my brother and his wife because they need a normal life, and you don't offer a normal life." He says, "Okay." And he doesn't go back. An anti-hero would have been loyal to his family. He would have gone back. So, Don Draper's not an anti-hero. He is extremely a complex, multi-dimensional, difficult human being, struggling somehow to find himself in the task of his life. There's nothing about him heroic.

Perhaps, the only thing about him that's heroic is his persistence. He'll go down to hell if he has to. He persists in trying to get an answer to what it means to live. He's trying to answer the question, "Who am I?" It's a great inspiration to realize the audience is with you in these difficult questions. If you write well, and you go into little chambers of hell that nobody has ever dared before, they'll go in there with you.

JOHN BUCHER: What are the scripts that every screenwriter should read?

ROBERT MCKEE: There is no good answer to that question. Suppose you're a comedy writer, and I say one of the greatest scripts ever written is Ingmar Bergman's *Through a Glass Darkly*. Why in the world would a comedy writer read that? If I say that *The Lady Eve* is a masterpiece of comedy writing, and you're trying to be the next Ingmar Bergman, why in the world would you read that? So there is no such thing as a set of screenplays that every writer should read. Every writer should read and study those films and TV series that really resonate with them as a human being. Everybody can create and should create their own list of what to read and study. Then, try to answer the questions, "How did this writer do that?" How did they get that character to that point? How did they put that question in my mind? How did they make me feel what I'm feeling now? Why do I care? How did they make me care?"

In addition you really should study bad screenplays and bad films. They are often more instructive than good scripts, because when you study bad screenplays

and bad movies, you ask yourself, "How did they
screw up?" Why is this so bad? What have they done
that's turned me off? Why don't you care? Why are
you not interested? Why do you feel you've seen all
this a thousand times? How could I have fixed that?
What would I do with this bad movie to turn it into
a better film? Force yourself to re-write bad movies
because when you're writing, your first draft will be a
bad movie. You can count on it. The first draft will be
terrible. The first thing you write is the worst thing you
will ever write, and you have to fix it. If you fix other
people's bad movies in your head, when you are guilty
of the same mistakes and the same failings, having
done that with other people, you can now look at your
own work and say, "My god, I did the same damn
dumb thing that I've seen in six films." But now you
have some idea what to do about it.

I'm always very suspicious and skeptical about people
who want models of greatness. I mean I think you
should look at these and answer those questions,
"How did this writer make this so wonderful?," and
that's certainly a learning experience, fine. But only
as a model of a standard against which you will judge
your own writing, not to copy. All I want people to do is
write something that's wonderful. And follow their own
sense of things, their own judgment and values and
perceptions and create something that will entertain,

grab my interest, hold me, and satisfy me.

TWO GREAT SHOWS
THAT TASTE GREAT TOGETHER:
THE WIRE, THE OFFICE, & THE LONELY WORLD

I've long been taken by the concept of ritual. For some, that word brings to mind images of secret societies, blood, and empty ceremony for ancient purposes. Ritual actually reinforces the stories we tell each other about who we are as a people. Ritual is still alive and well in the lives of Americans who sing "Happy Birthday" and blow out candles; wear white at weddings; gather as tribes (or families) on certain days of the year; watch certain movies, sports competitions, and eat certain foods on those days they gather; and even go to bed at the same time each night. On a psychological level, ritual reinforces that we are part of a group – that we are not alone. This is actually one of ritual's most powerful effects. It decreases loneliness.

Television has become the most significant ritualistic force in our lives, as it allows us to reinforce, alter, or retract the stories we tell about ourselves on a minute-by-minute basis. We may never know how great the role television has had in defining our story as humans. One thing we can be sure of: there is a seamless loop between our own stories that we see reflected on television and the television stories that reflect in our own lives.

I find a clear connection between two shows that have resonated deeply with audiences the past few decades – *The Office** and *The Wire*. Both shows reflect our story as Americans. However, the distance between the two is as far as the east from west. Yet both shows developed core audiences and have taken on even greater life since concluding their original broadcasts. Both shows, at their core, tackle the problem of loneliness.

In *The Office*, we see overt loneliness in the on-going dance between Pam and Jim. Dwight and Angela engage in a similar dance occasionally as well, as do Kelly and Ryan. Andy's relationship with Angela (and later Erin) evoke a certain loneliness as well. And dare we forget the ravenous love between Phyllis and Bob Vance of Vance Refrigeration. Perhaps the most significant exploration of loneliness, though, comes to us through Steve Carell's portrayal of Michael Scott.

Michael Scott is the picture of loneliness in America. He often makes his condition painfully obvious, while trying desperately to hide it from everyone in the office. Michael is constantly trying to get his co-workers to hang out with him outside of work. They form elaborate systems to avoid doing so. He inserts himself into wedding ceremonies, birthday celebrations, and lunchroom discussions—dying to connect with those he spends his time around. All the while, he seems aloof – not really understanding how much everyone is trying to avoid him. The only way we can avoid dealing with how much we relate is by laughing at him. We watch thinking of those we like to avoid, feeling better about ourselves and knowing that part of our collective story includes a chapter about people that *deserve* to be avoided.

In *The Wire*, loneliness takes different shadows. Drug dealers sit together in communal groups in front of government projects, homeless children take care of each other inside abandoned buildings, and police detectives find comfort in each other's beds. Even the most distinct example of an individual on the show, Omar Little, needs his lover, Brandon. Everyone on *The Wire* is trying to reconcile loneliness. It could be argued that the most important character on the show is Andre Royo's Reginald "Bubbles" Cousins. Bubbles comforts the loneliness of many characters – everyone from his fellow addict, Johnny Weeks, to the ethical stalwart, Kima Greggs. Bubbles is a symbol of hope throughout the show. He appears at moments when things seem most bleak, pushing his cart of white tees. He's a constant force and reminder that even when the world seems most empty, there is someone nearby. Bubbles serves as a reminder that refuges from loneliness are not perfect. His struggles with addiction were always a few feet away. But refuges are there. They do exist.

The Office takes work-place rituals to task while *The Wire* offers curious insights into the ever-changing rituals of the streets. But neither show forgets why we have rituals in the first place. They tell our stories. They tell stories of how we need each other regardless of the circumstances. There's a scene in *The Office* where Michael finally gets his wish. He is invited to Dave and Busters by his co-workers for an after-work get together. Over the course of the evening, he manages to remind everyone why they never invite him anywhere. The same situation often occurs at family get-togethers and office events. We are reminded exactly why we don't do this more often. An unkind word is said. A relative can't resist inserting their political views. A co-worker dominates the conversation with tales about his niece. Perhaps the greatest hope we find in ritualistic television is that the characters all force themselves to get together again later. They are intentional about their battles in fighting loneliness. We see them. If they can do it, maybe we can too.

* - For the sake of this piece, I focus on the American version of *The Office*. I am a fan of the original British vversion of the show. At some point, I might compare the British version to *The Wire* looking at the same problem of loneliness. I also intentionally focus on the "Michael Scott" years of *The Office,* as they seem the most concerned with loneliness.

3 FRAMEWORKS FOR BUILDING A STRONG STORY

There are an unlimited number of premises upon which a story can be based. Some stories are character-driven. Others are concept-driven. Others combine elements of both approaches. Regardless of which approach you begin your story with, you'll eventually encounter the other. If you begin with a concept, you'll eultimately have to work your way through developing the characters that will make the concept breathe. If you begin with a character, you'll have to, at some point, bring that protagonist through a journey at some point. Wherever your process begins, here are three frameworks for building a strong story around your character and the journey he or she will undertake.

An Ordinary Character Thrust Into An Extraordinary World

At some point in their career, most writers will tell the story of the "everyman." While humanity's earliest stories like *The Epic of Gilgamesh* told tales of extraordinary men, storytelling would eventually deliver to us a different sort of narrative: fairy tales. In these stories, we began to relate to the protagonists in ways we never had before. We could see ourselves in these characters. Fairy tales held up mirrors for us (*mirror, mirror on the wall),* while maintaining a sense of alluring whimsy, too. With landscapes often magical and distant, the characters were always familiar. And though the characters in these stories often weren't even given proper names (instead they were referred to as the huntsman in the woods, mother, or the evil witch, for example) they were *archetype*s to whom we couldn't help but relate.

Literature has used this method time and again. Countless stories are based on the situation that arises when an ordinary Alice is thrust into another world, passing through the looking glass. *Mirror, Mirror on the wall.* This method of drawing the audience in by telling the story of someone with a seemingly ordinary life – like their own - still works today.

We like to believe that our lives could hold adventure, just like the characters on the screen. In the midst of our mundane day, we hope the unexpected might happen, enchanted by the possibility of an exciting world lurking just around the corner. Stories about ordinary characters thrown into extraordinary worlds remind us of why we should keep our dreams alive.

In *Ex Machina*, an ordinary computer programmer wins a mysterious contest and is invited into the strange but exciting world of a futuristic mad scientist, driven to redefine what it means to be human. In many ways, it shares the same premise as other fabled tales of cinema where ordinary people are brought to a new world of danger and eccentricity. *The Wizard of Oz, Charlie and the Chocolate Factory*, and *Star Wars: A New Hope* are all included in the family of films that share this framework.

An Extraordinary Character Thrust Into An Ordinary World

Our culture has always been fascinated by extraordinary people. We've made heroes, celebrities, and even sideshow acts out of those with characteristics or talents that reach outside the norm. Numerous stories are built around the idea of how these extraordinary people function in our ordinary world. Audiences have flocked to watch geniuses such as John Nash (*A Beautiful Mind*) and Alan Turing (*The Imitation Game*) overcome their struggles with the very ordinary world around them. We wonder how Wolfgang Amadeus Mozart (*Amadeus*) and Mark Zuckerberg (*The Social Network*) will deal with the jealousy surrounding them in our all too ordinary world.

Perhaps the genre that most clearly presents this framework is the superhero film. How can a man others call "super" have a life put into our "less than super" world? What will be the outcome when the extraordinary Tony Stark (from *Avengers: Age of Ultron*) tries to breathe new life into a dead peacekeeping program, only to have it go awry, entangling him with an extraordinary villain called Ultron? While many stories of the extraordinary leave a trail of broken hearts, damaged egos, and exploding buildings, this is not always the case. This framework has also served as the basis for films like *Forrest Gump*, *The Waterboy*, and the journey Will Ferrell's Buddy takes in the holiday classic, *Elf*. The key to this framework is the arc that the audience experiences while watching the story. We come to recognize that these extraordinary people are much more like us than we first realized.

An Ordinary Character Trying To Cope With An Ordinary World

This is the most difficult of the frameworks to execute. We risk boring the audience. Usually now reserved for the independent film market, stories featuring an ordinary character trying to cope with their life in an ordinary world must be driven by fascinating personas exploring an internal journey more significant than their external one. Richard Linklater's *Boyhood* mastered this delicate balance. The television classic, *Seinfeld*, brilliantly made comedy gold out of this framework. The premise has served multiple Oscar winners including *American Beauty*, *Ordinary People*, and *Kramer vs. Kramer*.

The key to this framework is quality writing and extremely gifted actors that can execute complex emotional movement over time. This is a framework that should only be attempted by the experienced, developed writer. Many who lack the skill to orchestrate this sort of advanced storytelling have left audiences yawning, zoning out, or worse – leaving the theater.

Have an idea for a story? Currently working on a script? Is yours the story of an ordinary character in extraordinary circumstances? Or is it the story of an extraordinary character in an otherwise ordinary world? Perhaps you feel comfortable enough to attempt the story of an ordinary character coping with their ordinary world. Regardless of which framework best suits your situation and vision, seek out the family of films that have used that same premise. Watch them closely. Notice what worked and what didn't. Do certain rules or patterns emerge across the films? Learning as we follow the paths of those who've went before us can prevent weeks of frustration and wasted time.

PLATONIC STORYTELLING: 3 GREEK MYTHS THAT WILL IMPROVE YOUR WRITING

Many writers realize later in life that they should have paid more attention in high school. One of the most significant subjects you might have slept through was Greek mythology. Knowing the classical tales that have undergirded Western culture is actually one of the most powerful tools a writer can have. Understanding why these myths have endured for thousands of years helps us better craft our contemporary stories around human psychology and problem solving.

There are overt adaptations of Greek myths such as *Thor* and *Clash of the Titans*. *O Brother, Where Art Thou?* received a great deal of press as a modern take on Homer's *Odyssey*. Much has also been written about mythological metaphors in most superhero films. However, reading some of the lesser-known myths from Greek mythology can provide insight into archetypes and tropes we have seen throughout the history of storytelling. Finding a new take or modern approach on these narratives and characters might just be the hook you need for that new script you are writing. Here are three Greek myths worth checking out.

Pygmalion

Ovid's narrative poem, *Metamorphoses*, metions a mythical sculptor from Cypress named Pygmalion, who falls in love with a statue he creates. Pygmalion prays to Aphrodite for a bride who would be "the living likeness of my ivory girl." He later kisses the lips of his statue and finds them warm. The sculpture comes to life. Aphrodite has granted his wish. There are a variety of takes and cinematic reinterpretations of the story of Pygmalion. Professor Henry Higgins teaches Eliza Doolittle how to function in high society, and thus his creation comes to life, in *My Fair Lady*. Edward Lewis does the same for Vivian Ward in *Pretty Woman*. *Weird Science, Mannequin, The Mighty Aphrodite*, and *Ruby Sparks* all follow similar story lines. However, one added element to most modern interpretations of Pygmalion is that the "creation" ends up bringing just as much meaning to the life of the "creator." We find variations of the Pygmalion story in tales ranging from *Pinocchio* to *Eddie the Eagle*.

Oedipus Rex

This Athenian tragedy, written by Sophocles around 420 BCE, has influenced writers and thinkers from Yeats to Freud, and filmmakers from Welles to Nolan. The story of a man destined to kill his father and marry his mother, *Oedipus Rex* popularized dark aspects of the human psyche that we still wrestle with today. In *Back to the Future*, Marty McFly must fight an Oedipus-type situation where his mother seeks a romantic relationship with him, unknowingly supplanting his father. *The Star Wars* saga is filled with Oedipus imagery. Anakin Skywalker loses his mother, who he seems obsessed with, finding love with an older woman who looks much like her. His mother's death is a key element that drives him to the Dark Side. Luke Skywalker unknowingly seeks to destroy his father in the story and enjoys a romantic kiss with a female family member, also unbeknownst to him. *Monster-in-Law, Cyrus, Failure to Launch*, and *Psycho* all feature men who just can't seem to get over their mothers. *Sons of Anarchy* puts a different spin on the *Oedipus Rex* narrative, presenting a protagonist that lionizes his father and murders his mother. Even the recent, *Batman vs. Superman: Dawn of Justice* takes a spin on the mother/son theme.

Persephone and Demeter

In this Greek classic, Persephone, daughter of Zeus and Demeter, is abducted by Hades, god of the underworld. There are a number of variations of the story. However, one element always present is that after she is rescued, Persephone still returns to the underworld once a year to rule as queen for a season. Different myths speak of Persephone's reluctance or sometimes great willingness to make this journey. Regardless, when Persephone is in the underworld, her mother, Demeter - goddess of harvest, refuses to let the crops grow, which is why we have winter. Stories of women descending into the underworld for a season have occupied literature and films since these mediums were created. In *Silence of the Lambs*, Clarice Starling literally descends a flight of stairs into a dark underworld, where Hannibal Lecter awaits to lead her on her journey. In both *The Matrix Reloaded* and *The Matrix Revolutions,* a character named Persephone is the wife of the Merovingian, a Hades-like figure in the underworld of The Matrix, seen lounging in Club Hel. *10 Cloverfield Lane, The Hateful Eight, Mad Max: Fury Road*, And *Fifty Shades of Grey* all feature women, connected to controlling men, who descend into one type of underworld or another.

It's easy to get run after the latest trends as writers. Sometimes, we get caught up in chasing what seems to be selling at the moment. It's important to remember that the most enduring story elements, archetypes, and plots rarely seem to change. It's the worlds in which we set them and the characters we invent that make these timeless tropes seem new. When you plan your summer reading this year, throw a few Greek classics in the mix. You might be surprised at all the ways your writing will improve.

STRAIGHT OUTTA REALITY:
3 GUIDING PRINCIPLES FOR ADAPTING STORIES
FROM ACTUAL EVENTS

True Stories have fascinated audiences since the early days of storytelling. Knowing a story is based on actual events sparks interest in films that might never draw the curiosity of the average moviegoer. These stories and their themes carry the weight of truth, and though truth can certainly be explored and examined in fictional narrative, it's not always found or presented as powerfully. It's the reason so many films now begin with a text card informing us that what we are about to see is based on something that really did occur.

With films such as *Straight Outta Compton* and *The End of the Tour* having box office success, you might be compelled to bring your own real life story to the screen. The Academy Awards have always been friendly to such stories. It's no wonder that writers who hear of or experience dramatic events often desire to adapt them into scripts. Here are three guiding principles for adapting stories from real life.

SIMPLIFY
Combine characters and events while compressing space and time

In *The Wolf of Wall Street*, Jonah Hill's character, Donnie Azoff, is a composite of several characters from the protagonist's real life. In *Dallas Buyer's Club*, Ron Woodroof's diagnosis of AIDS occurs in one dramatic moment but in reality, doctors informed Woodroof about the possible diagnosis over a period of several years. The film's other central characters,

Rayon and Dr. Eve Saks, are also composites. The
creation of Rayon gives Woodroof a specific challenge
in overcoming his prejudices while facing the disease.
In *Saving Mr. Banks*, Pamela Travers plays cat and
mouse with Walt Disney to negotiate the details of
bringing her *Mary Poppins* story to the screen. While
Travers did visit the U.S., the negotiations surrounding
the story took place over a number of years. Walt never
flew to London to seal the deal. However, the events
that actually took place were less than dramatic. In
order for the story to work, the writer had to compress
the timeline and put the protagonist and antagonist in
the same physical space, rather than have the conflict
worked out through telegrams and letters.

FOCUS
Concentrate on themes, not just details

Some details make a story feel authentic. Other details
are distracting. There was a great deal of controversy
surrounding events that were omitted from the film,
A Beautiful Mind. The story's central character, John
Nash, fathered a child before he met his wife Alicia,
who is pictured in the film. Nash refused to support
his son and neglected the boy as well as the woman
who bore him. The narrative in *A Beautiful Mind*,
is arguably Alicia's story of tenacity in an unwieldy
relationship, which wouldn't necessitate those darker
details from Nash's life. This is one of many omissions
and changes the scriptwriter felt necessary to enforce
the theme of the film.

We must remember that we are not documentarians.
We are storytellers. And a story should not be judged
on its historical accuracy but rather its ability to

engage an audience. Lee Daniels' *The Butler* came under similar attack for historical inaccuracies. In the film, the central character appears to dislike Presidents Richard Nixon and Ronald Reagan. The real Eugene Allen (named Cecil Gaines in the film) has actually spoken fondly of both men in interviews. However, the portrayal in the film is meant to reinforce the difficulties of people of color under those administrations. The writers have spoken about the relationship being metaphorical and symbolic, rather than literal.

The King's Speech is admittedly inaccurate in many of its details. For good reason, stories like this claim to be only *based* on real events. The theme of the film deals with the role of friendship in overcoming obstacles. The creators chose to omit and alter history to reinforce the themes they wanted to tackle. Many of the historical details are either irrelevant to their theme or would simply bore their audience. *Story* was king in *The King's Speech* and audiences responded.

DARE
Don't be afraid to change what actually happened

When adapting real-life events, we cannot be afraid to completely change what might have actually happened for the sake of the story. Many times when workshopping scripts based on actual events, often from their own lives, writers will insist that a note is not valid because it's not *what happened* in real life. Real life must always take a back seat to good storytelling when adapting for the screen.

Lincoln doesn't try to encapsulate the American president's life, but only depicts the last few weeks. Spielberg and the film's other creators made great efforts to be historically accurate. However, one of the most emotional scenes of the film involves Thaddeus Stevens and his lover, a person of color, at the end of the film. While Stevens was accused of having a relationship with his housekeeper by his anti-abolitionist critics, there's no actual evidence it was true. However, it gives us a compelling backstory for his character and offers a potential motivation for the hard work Stevens offers to the cause. In *American Sniper*, Chris Kyle enlists in the military after finding his girlfriend in bed with another man and seeing American lives lost on the news. In actuality, there's no record of either of those events occurring. He had always intended to enlist after high school. However, these fictional details help give us a stronger reason for our hero to go on his journey and provide a logical through line where real life didn't necessarily offer that.

While these examples can be swept away as minor details in the given narrative, there are many more significant examples of history being altered for the sake of a better story. For instance, Alan Turing single-handedly invents and physically builds a machine that breaks the Germans' Enigma code in *The Imitation Game*. This simply wasn't true. The machine Turing "invents" in the film was actually created by Polish cryptanalysts before Turing was even working for the British government. Turing's innovation was actually designing a modified machine that broke codes faster by looking for likely letter combinations and ruling out others. Mathematician, Gordon Welchman, partnered intimately with Turing to create the design, but is not mentioned in the film. A similar critique was launched against the film *Captain Phillips* and the diminished heroic role of others in the story. Do these historical changes weaken the films? Not at all. They make their stories stronger. The changes allow us to focus on the journey of a singular character, without getting into convoluted details about contributions the audience won't likely care about. Our hero in the film is who matters and the story is better for the changes.

MAKING IT REAL:
3 LESSONS FROM DOCUMENTARY STORYTELLING

For many years, documentaries were not a form of storytelling enjoyed by mass audiences. Occasionally, a musical documentary of interest to viewers would break through the sea of science and educational fare that ruled the genre. A few decades ago, all that changed. Documentaries have become one of the most exciting and engaging forms of storytelling in our culture.

In a natural progression, this form has moved from the big screen to serialized storytelling. HBO's documentary series *The Jinx* and Netflix's *Making A Murderer* have been the subjects of much discussion around the water cooler this year. Here are three characteristics of documentary storytelling that should be found in any strong narrative, regardless of genre.

Stories Are About Characters

There have been two approaches to incorporating characters into documentary storytelling. The first is to feature the subjects of the doc as characters themselves. Many documentaries have been created around fascinating people whose stories are compelling, sometimes odd, but true. *Amy* tells the story of Amy Winehouse, a character that many were familiar with but a person that many were not. *Soaked In Bleach* and *Cobain: Montage of Heck* both feature Kurt Cobain, revealing aspects of his humanity never before seen. Focused on a more uplifting character, *He Named Me Malala* tells the story of the young woman who was shot for standing up to the Taliban.

The Wolfpack tells the story of a talented band of brothers kept from society who found a way to express themselves through their imaginations and overcome the massive challenges they faced. The men in this story rival any fictional characters that have ever been created. In *Finders Keepers*, we see an eclectic duo fighting over the right to own a human foot. Truth really can be stranger than fiction.

The second method is to feature the documentarian as the story's main character. In these stories, the filmmaker enjoys a great deal of screen time, as is the case with Michael Moore and Russell Brand's. However, sometimes the filmmaker is not seen at all, but rather lets their perspective and point of view drive the story, as is the case with Rashida Jones's *Hot Girls Wanted*.

Conflict Is Essential

The single element found in modern documentaries, differentiating them from the docs of the past, is the heightened level of conflict. For years, the central conflict of this genre was non-human. Lions battled gazelles. Elephants fought to protect their young. However, it wasn't until human stakes were introduced that larger audiences began showing up for these stories. *3 ½ Minutes, Ten Bullets* looks at the state of racism in our country through the lens of a single incident involving the shooting of a young black man. *Cartel Land* explores the murderous landscape of the drug trade in Mexico. Rape crimes on college campuses are taken to task in *The Hunting Ground*. While life and death are not quite the stakes in *All Things Must Pass: The Rise and Fall of Tower Records*, the conflict is just is real. Watching the destruction of cultural artifacts under the boots of our ever-progressing technology strikes an emotional chord in many people.

Aristotle once suggested that there were only five conflicts available to us in storytelling: man could battle another man, nature, society, himself, or what we have come to call "the machine." Even today, most compelling stories, documentary or narrative, focus on one of these conflicts.

Set Ups And Payoffs Hold The Audience

Many people have good ideas for cinematic stories. It's the execution where most fall flat. Learning how to set up scenes followed by "payoff" is an art form all to its self. A strong documentary is paced with inhales and exhales just like a narrative feature. Sometimes, these set ups include letting the audience in on a secret or a joke before the characters in the story are aware of it. Other times, the set up might include an insignificant person, place, or line of dialogue that rises to importance later in the story. In *Thought Crimes: The Case of the Cannibal Cop*, we watch setup after setup leading to whether the payoff will include a verdict of guilty or innocent. In *The Resurrection of Jake the Snake Roberts*, we see set-ups that provide opportunities for Jake. Some of the payoffs include positive outcomes for Roberts and others do not. Essentially, the movie is a set up to see whether the wrestler can get his life together by the film's conclusion. With serialized documentary storytelling, it is of utmost importance that each episode end with a setup that will bring the audience back next time for the pay off.

Many people are surprised to learn that most documentaries are scripted once the footage has been captured. The elements that make docs strong, interesting, and compelling are the same elements that we have access to as scriptwriters. Learning how to use the tools we are familiar with as well as how to develop new tools strengthens our skills as writers and storytellers. So, go watch a doc. It just might improve that script you've been working on.

THE BIG SECRET:
3 SECRETS YOUR CHARACTER MUST KEEP TO SURVIVE

In an age where *everything* about *everybody* somehow finds its way online, what we manage to keep to ourselves has become more and more difficult. Secrets are a universal human characteristic. We've all had one. We've all let one slip. Creating realistic characters requires creating their secrets as well. But secrets can be tricky. We need to empathize with *why* the character is keeping their secret but the secret can't make us hate the character either. Some secrets are despicable and hurt others more than they hurt the keeper of the undisclosed truth. A character's secret should be honorable or at least redeemable, once it is revealed. In essence, a secret is a lie, and if a character is going to lie, we need to believe that we would tell the same lie in an identical situation. Here are three secrets your character should be able to keep.

The Friendly Secret

Some secrets are kept for the benefit of others. We keep the truth hidden to protect those we value. Technically lies, friendly secrets are usually honorable and we admire the characters who keep them. In *Creed*, Rocky Balboa keeps Adonis's father's identity a secret because he understands the desire to build one's own reputation and not ride the coat tails of another's success. In *Mad Max: Fury Road*, Furiosa sneaks four women out of a treacherous situation and keeps their secret, not for her own benefit, but because she believes in a greater cause. Poe Dameron keeps a droid's location secret, even at the threat of torture, for the benefit of the Republic in *The Force Awakens*. And though we might disagree with his politics, Rudolf Abel keeps Russia's secrets in *Bridge of Spies* – a dangerous move that might cost him his life.

The Selfish Secret

Many secrets we keep because they benefit us directly. Our characters should be no different. However, we must be careful in executing secrets of this nature. If a secret is *too* selfish, the audience might not empathize with the character when the secret is revealed. At the core of the secret should be something universally understandable or even beautiful. Carol Aird keeps her love for Therese Belivet a secret to protect her relationship with her daughter in *Carol*. Dalton Trumbo keeps his identity secret as he continues to write award-winning films in order to stay true to himself while feeding his family in *Trumbo*. Daniel Hillard dresses up as *Mrs. Doubtfire* so he can spend more time with his children. Michael Dorsey dresses up as *Tootsie* to get a much-needed job. As part of her job, Josie Geller goes incognito as a high school student in *Never Been Kissed*. All these examples are noble reasons to hide a secret. However, sometimes characters keep secrets that are less than noble, but we can understand because perhaps we, too, have shared the embarrassment they feel. In *Rushmore*, Max Fischer tells people his father is a brain surgeon, when in actuality he is a barber. We understand that sometimes children keep secrets in order to make themselves look more important – and some never grow out of this habit. In *Magnolia*, Frank T.J. Mackey keeps his past a secret because of the pain and embarrassment it caused him. Most of us have some

event in our past we would like to keep out of view as
well.

The Scary Secret

While the specific reasons for secret-keeping
outnumber the stars, at the core of many of these
reasons is fear. Some secrets are scary. We hide them
out of trepidation. While knowing the truth might be a
huge weight to bear, the revelation of that truth could
cause even greater danger. Bridger carries a terrible
secret in *The Revenant* – not over something he has
done, but over something he saw happen. The entire
plot of *Spotlight* revolves around the uncovering of
secrets in The Catholic Church. Several characters
in this film live in fear of their secrets being exposed.
Virtually every character in *The Hateful Eight* is
carrying a secret, too. The story is built around what
secrets are revealed when, and by whom.

The creativity in a story will come largely from why a
character keeps a secret and what that secret is. And
one element should always be present: the secret must
come out. We can squirm with the character as they
duck and dodge the truth, but in the end, the secret
must surface. That's where the drama is. We must see
the character face what they feared most. In real life,
secrets can go to the grave, but in the world of story,
they must have their day in the sun.

BUILDING A LAUNCHPAD:
3 STARTING PLACES FOR YOUR CHARACTER'S
INTERNAL JOURNEY

One of the most difficult puzzles a writer must solve involves the relationship between the inner needs and external goal of their protagonist. Some writers pitch stories solely about a character that *learns* or *comes to realize* something, not recognizing this is impossible to capture and represent on film since it occurs inside someone's head. Other writers pitch stories of characters that risk life and limb to bring back a treasure from the underworld with no internal lessons or realizations along the way. As a wise man once said, we must restore balance to the force. Good storytelling emphasizes the internal development of a protagonist that results from the external journey he or she experiences. However, before a character can learn or realize anything, we must establish that there is something they *need* to learn or realize. Here are three places from where your character's internal journey can launch.

The Place Of Inexperience

Many journeys begin with a character that lacks the skills or maturity to carry out the task they are given. Over the course of the story, the protagonist must face trials that will bring about their growth. They must be trained by those who possess the knowledge they don't have. The only way to gain the experience they need to complete their external goal is to slay the dragon that stands in their path. The dragon lives inside of them and usually goes by the name Ego. Once slain, the wisdom our protagonist craves is bestowed upon them.

They can now complete the external mission they set out on, but more importantly they now hold the *secret* they need should that dragon's twin brother ever cross their path. While the language of explaining these journeys is dramatic and often mythic, the principles apply across genres. In *Real Genius,* Mitch is the smartest guy at the school, but he lacks the experience he needs to complete the academic gauntlet ahead of him without losing his mind. Throughout the course of the story, he gains the social skills he lacks to get the girl, survives jealous competitors, and saves the world in the process. Luke Skywalker can only destroy the Death Star when he abandons his ego and need for control in *Star Wars: A New Hope.* He closes his eyes, uses the force, and is able to save the galaxy. *The Karate Kid, Rocky,* and *Dodgeball* feature characters who journey from inexperienced to experienced.

The Place Of Selfishness

This journey can be slightly more difficult to execute in that we still need to root for the protagonist, despite their selfishness. This can get tricky. We must show the need for the character to grow in the first act. However, we also must show that this is a character worth getting behind. While challenging, this can be accomplished through humor, charm, or by making the protagonist appear simply misunderstood. In *Bruce Almighty*, Bruce finally realizes that he wants Grace to be happy more than he wants her back in his life. Only then is he given the chance to reunite with her – once his ego has been slain. Bill Murray's character becomes a better human being when he turns loose of his selfishness and realizes life should be shared with others in *St. Vincent*. In *Pretty Woman,*

Richard Gere becomes the best version of himself only after he releases his arrogance and admits his true feelings for Julia Roberts' character. *Field of Dreams*, *The Descendants*, and *Dallas Buyers Club* all feature characters going on this journey from arrogance or selfishness to humility and love.

The Place Of Independence

One of the most common themes in film echoes our deep need for each other. We can't solve the riddle without help. We can't win the fight without someone to train us. We can't be our best selves without others. Many character archetypes exist for this purpose of making our protagonist into the person they need to be. The mentor, the wise old sage, the sidekick, and the lover all are perfect foils for our protagonists' independence. *Erin Brockovich* can't defeat the evil corporate empire without Albert Finney and Aaron Eckhart. Ben Affleck can't complete his journey without Jason Lee in *Chasing Amy*. And even *Ferris Bueller* can't have his day off unless Cameron comes and picks him up in his car. Films like *Crash* focus on this deep need for one another thematically, while *The Blind Side*, *The American President*, and *Jerry Maguire* all focus more directly on this idea. These films remind us to recognize the important role of others in our lives; we must welcome others if we are to accomplish the personal missions to which we've been called.

3 STORIES THAT SHOULD NEVER BE TOLD

Everyone has a story. In the business of storytelling, we often spend a great deal of time teasing out stories from people's lives, historical moments, and universally relatable situations. But, have you ever given any thought to what stories should never be told? Are there any stories that are just off limits? Some of the best stories push boundaries and press the edges of our conscious reality, so where is the line? How can we identify a problematic premise before we even begin to put words on a page? Here are three stories that you should stop writing before you even get started.

The Story with the Heavy-Handed Agenda

There's an old saying that originated in the Golden Age of Hollywood – if you have a message, call Western Union. Of course, messages aren't sent via telegram anymore, but the sentiment is one that Hollywood is still sensitive to. Since creators first began to recognize the immense power films had over audiences, people have been using them to advance philosophies, sell products, and persuade opinion. The tricky aspect of all this is that a well-told story should have a definite world view. Storytellers need to have an opinion about the universe and the way things should be. The balance is found is the subtlety of the art form. Films are better at asking questions than providing answers. We can introduce difficult issues or themes into our stories without being *prescriptive* as to how characters must deal with them. Being *descriptive* about the truths that underpin these situations is a more effective and impactful goal to strive for. Allowing an audience to make their own discoveries is part of the cinematic, narrative journey. Life is full of gray matters. If our stories can't reflect this, they will feel less than authentic. *Calvary*, *Brooklyn*, and *Sicario* all presented important cultural issues and stories without agendas or being too heavy-handed.

The Story That Isn't Thematically Or Emotionally True

Often a personal experience that leads us to our own agenda can blind us to the fact that we are telling a story that is thematically or emotionally untrue. Hard work always pays off. Simple anecdotal ideas like this can seem like a good theme to tackle in a story. Many times, this phrase *does* hold true. However, many times it does not. Some people work very hard for years and never see many fruits for the labors. Ask most screenwriters. The more accurate statement or theme may be that hard work pays off in ways that don't always include financial or traditional successes, even if sometimes it does. In a story exploring this theme, it may be important to showcase a character for whom hard work does not pay off in a traditional way, as well as a character for whom it does. *Me and Earl and the Dying Girl*, *Steve Jobs*, and *Whiplash* all avoid easy themes and emotions that aren't always authentic for more difficult characters and stories that are both thematically and emotionally true.

The Story That Doesn't Respect The Audience

Just about all of us struggle with being lazy in some area or another. Our current media culture often makes it easy for audiences to be lazy as well. But as this "golden age" of television has proved, there exists an army of people who do not want to be spoon fed when it comes to their stories. Spoon feeding an audience can take on many forms. It may involve over-simplifying a complex issue, demonizing a character with a multifaceted worldview, or any number of methods that involve subtle ways of treating the audience like they are stupid. This can be a very tempting opportunity for even the savviest storyteller when we have a point we are trying to drive home or a complicated issue to tease out with a very short amount of time to do it in.

Great writers learn to be efficient with their words, descriptions, and scenes, especially when writing for the screen. But being aware of when you've crossed the line into melodrama or over-simplification is essential. Overcoming a disease as nuanced as alcoholism in a five-minute story or even a two hour-story isn't usually believable. It's disrespectful to audience members who have fought with this issue personally, as well as those who have been impacted by it.

A key component of a good character arc is that a character actually be *capable* of change. A character cannot just wake up one morning and decide not to be schizophrenic. If your protagonist battles this condition, it might be wiser to make your story about one small goal the character is able to accomplish in their journey as opposed to overcoming something as massive as mental illness. Even audiences who have never wrestled with such issues will resist the convenience and unbelievability of full recovery in these stories. We tend to recognize truth when we see it. Those of us who have *experienced* certain truths will insist that storytellers shy away from truths they have only heard rumor of. *Philomena, Short Term 12,* and *Silver Linings Playbook* all found audiences by refusing to spoon feed them. We would do well to learn from the risks and brave approaches each of those films took.

A TRIBUTE TO MELISSA MATHISON:
3 STORY SECRETS IN E.T.

The screenwriting world lost a titan of our industry on November 4, 2015. Melissa Mathison passed away at the age of 65 on November 4. Having written legendary scripts like *The Black Stallion* and *Kundun* for Martin Scorsese, most people will remember Mathison for her greatest storytelling achievement – E.T. The Extra-Terrestrial. For several years, Steven Spielberg had wanted to tell a story about a boy and an alien, loosely based on the imaginary friend he created to cope with his parents divorce, for several years. He was a fan of Mathison's work on *The Black Stallion* but had not considered her to pen his new story until fate intervened. Spielberg ran into Mathison on the set of *Raiders of the Lost Ark* in Tunisia. She was there visiting her boyfriend, who would later become her husband, Harrison Ford. Speilberg felt it was a sign that Mathison was the person to write his next film. Between takes on *Raiders*, he undertook the slow process of convincing Mathison to take the job. She eventually accepted the offer and knocked out a first draft of *E.T. and Me* in eight weeks. The rest, we can safely say, is history. Besides being one of the most beloved stories in all of cinema, *E.T.* is also an excellently constructed script. Here are three story secrets that lie inside the film.

The Subtext Drives The Story

Discussion about the loss of Elliot's father is only given a few moments of screen time. We quickly learn that the father has left the family and has a new girlfriend. The two of them are away on a Mexican vacation. This affects each member of the family in different ways.

Elliot's mother is upset. His brother, Michael, wants to cover up the reality of the situation and is distraught with Elliot for bringing it up. Gertie, Elliot's sister, is too young to understand the nuances of the moment but can clearly sense things are wrong. Elliot, himself, is lost. He's without a guide. He needs a father. He needs a friend. This subtext of Elliot's need for a father drives the story of *E.T.* It's what helps Elliot overcome his initial fear of the alien. It's what motivates him to help E.T. get home, despite the loss he will suffer in the process. It's what drives him to involve his family to rally around this unifying figure. While he never appears on screen, Elliot's father could be considered the most important character in the story, as it is he that creates the hole all other characters will attempt to fill. Mathison was building on a grand tradition of subtexts involving strained relationships between fathers and their children. Treasured films would carry on the tradition in *The Empire Strikes Back*, *The Royal Tenenbaums*, and *The Judge*.

Supporting Characters Provide The Heart Of The Story

Elliot knew he couldn't, on his own, help get E.T. back home on his own. The characters who surround our protagonist play important roles in helping complete the plan. His older brother, Michael, is a reluctant participant at first. However, over the course of the story, his character experiences his own range of feelings about the alien living in their home. This becomes a metaphor for the "aliened" brother who has bee living in his home for years. The reality of this truth is not lost on Michael and we see him treat Elliot differently by the end of the film. Though the middle child, Elliot emerges as the leader of his broken family in the final scene of the movie. His family humbly acknowledges this. Elliot's sister, Gertie, allows us to step into her shoes as she overcomes her initial fear of E.T. As she becomes playful with the new family friend, we find ourselves rooting for the alien and his need to return home. As Gertie changes her feelings about E.T., we follow suit. Unless our hero has people to care about – people he cares about losing – the audience may fail to care themselves.

Death & Resurrection Themes Are Universal

There are a number of deaths and resurrections in E.T., both literal and metaphorical. This theme is one of the most powerful in all of cinema and can play out multiple times in the same story. Elliot's family has experienced a metaphorical death at the beginning of the film, having lost their father. The family will never be whole again. Somehow, over the course of the story, E.T. manages to resurrect the family with the magic he brings. We find them once again whole in the film's final image.

There is also a death of innocence in the story. Because of the father's leaving, the family has lost its collective innocence, in a sense. Each member of the family, but especially Elliot, must now escalate his maturity. Getting E.T. back home, depends on this. Keeping E.T. a secret requires the death of innocent truth in order to succeed. But in the end, the death of innocence is rewarded with a new innocence – a pure honesty within the family about what they've been through and who they are.

There is also the literal physical death of E.T. near the end of the second act of the story. Elliot mourns the loss of his friend. We believe all is truly lost now. The mission has failed. No one will ever be complete again. But somehow the miraculous emerges. The warm glow of E.T.'s heart illuminates his plastic coffin. He lives again. He has experienced resurrection. Film ranging from *Birdman* to *Patch Adams* to *The Lord of the Rings* all enforce this universal theme of death and the astonishing power to rise again.

Melissa Mathison's final script, *The BFG*, based on the novel by Roald Dahl, premiered in theaters in 2016. Steven Spielberg directed.

SAY MY NAME:
3 THEORIES FOR NAMING CHARACTERS IN YOUR STORIES

As briefly mentioned earlier, fairy tales and fables were often written about characters without specific names. Stories about a nameless old woman who lived in the woods, a country mouse who visited the city, or a young girl whose mother had died were quite common. These stories left their protagonists unnamed so that the audience might insert themselves into the story. These, to remind, were stories about the "everyman" or "everywoman." In our current culture of storytelling, we name our characters, often with great intention. Many writers go as far as to avoid character names that end in "s" because of the awkwardness that can arise when you write the possessive form of that name. Here are a few other theories about naming characters in your story.

Literal Theory

With Literal Theory, the character's name literally translates to something else in another language, dialect, or form. *Cinderella* comes from the French word *Cendrillon* meaning "little ashes." Sherlock is an English surname meaning "shear lock" or short hair. We can assume that Arthur Conan Doyle used the name with the intention that the character never lets things get out of hand. He keeps things under control.

While *Finding Nemo* is arguably Marlin's story, Nemo means "nobody" in Latin, giving us greater insight into the inner journey of these characters. Cluing us in to a reveal no one saw coming, Darth Vader is a play on

dark *vater*, which is German for father. *Harry Potter*'s
Albus Dumbledore translates to "white bumblebee" in
Old English – something the character hints at with
his penchant for humming. Perhaps the most prolific
user of Literal Theory was J.R.R. Tolkien. While his
extensive use of dead European language could fill an
entire volume, a few brief examples include: Samwise,
which is "half wise" in Old English, Gandalf, which is
"wand elf" in Old Norse, and Frodo, deriving from the
Germanic element, *frod*, which means wise.

Semiotic Theory

In Semiotic Theory, the character's name is a sign or
symbol for something else. Some avoid this theory,
fearing it's a bit on the nose. However, its long history
throughout literature as well as its current use makes
it a theory we can't ignore. In *San Andreas*, Dwayne
Johnson's character is named Ray – a ray of hope in
a bleak situation. Multitudes of movies have called
their female characters Rose, Joy, Violet, or Angelica
to symbolize her feminine traits. In *Angel Heart*, Robert
De Niro's Satan is cleverly named Louis Cyphre, while
Mickey Rourke plays Harry Angel.

The *Star Wars* films often use this theory with
character names like Luke Skywalker and Han Solo.
In addition to Literal Theory, the *Harry Potter* films
also draw on semiotic theory with characters such
as Remus Lupin and Sirius Black. Remus and his
twin brother Romulus were abandoned as babies and
raised by wolves according to legends surrounding
the founding of Rome. Lupin refers to someone who
can take on the form of a wolf through concentration
while retaining his or her human intelligence. Sirius,

of course, refers to the "dog star" which is the brightest in the Canis Major (or Great Dog) constellation. The use of Semiotic Theory in television runs rampant as well. An examination of *Breaking Bad*'s Walter White/ Heisenberg could alone easily fill another article.

Chaos Theory

With Chaos Theory, character names seem believable, without significance, random, and perhaps common at first glance, but somehow still capture the feel or essence of the individual. While originally named Indiana Smith after George Lucas's dog, it's hard to imagine a more perfect name for an adventurer than Indiana Jones. There's nothing in the name that speaks to the exotic, yet somehow it just feels right. The same might be said of Jack Reacher, Hannibal Lecter, and Sarah Conner.

In the recent *Jurassic World*, we see characters like Owen Grady, Claire Dearing, and Vic Hoskins (portrayed by Chris Pratt, Bryce Dallas Howard, Vincent D'Onofrio respectively). Again, the names don't seem to have any symbolism or literalism. They just feel right. They feel like they capture the character. The same can be said of Cameron Crowe's characters in *Aloha* with names such as Brian Gilcrest, Woody Woodside, and Carson Welch, played by Bradley Cooper, John Krasinski, and Bill Murray. When using Chaos Theory to name your characters, you have to go with your gut. Sit with the name. See how it feels when you say it aloud. You'll know when you've perfectly captured the character you've been building.

DARK DESIRES: 3 THINGS YOUR ANTAGONIST MUST WANT

Despite the fact that many stories pit heroes against non-human forces as their central point of conflict, the vast majority of stories throughout history have been about a hero fighting a single human antagonist. For every *San Andreas* (man vs. nature) or *Jurassic World* (man vs. monster), there are 10 films that focus on the struggle between two people – one who wins and another who loses.

When asked, most people assume the antagonist desires whatever the protagonist doesn't. The problem with this approach is that both characters could potentially achieve their goals at some point in the story without having to battle at all – or even be in the same room. The most powerful stories are about heroes who want something and enemies that want the exact same thing. Only one can walk away with the prize. Here are three types of stories that will force your hero and your antagonist into the same physical space to fight for a single goal.

The Contest

Narratives about sports or athletic contests have a long, rich history in film. Structurally, these stories can be easier to tell, because they naturally lead to a final battle in the third act, where both protagonist and antagonist occupy one confined space, and only one will emerge the winner. While most of these tales conclude with our protagonist on top (*The Karate Kid*, *Hoosiers*, and *The Mighty Ducks*), it can be just as powerful to see the antagonist as the victor (*Rocky*,

Friday Night Lights, Tin Cup, Million Dollar Baby, Coach Carter). While these stories often do center on sports, there are many other types of contests that match a hero against an antagonist (*Pitch Perfect 2, Election, Slumdog Millionaire*).

The Treasure Hunt

In one sense, stories about a treasure hunt are a play on sports contest stories, in that they are a race toward a finish line. Indiana Jones and the Nazis are both racing toward their goal of the lost ark. Robert Langdon and a secret Catholic order are both racing toward the Holy Grail in *The Da Vinci Code. Romancing the Stone, Lord of the Rings, The Goonies*, and the *National Treasure* films also revolve around a similar premise.

Sometimes, however, the treasure is a person. In *Titanic*, the treasure is Rose. In *Sixteen Candles*, the treasure is Jake Ryan. In *Django Unchained*, the treasure is Django's wife. Often, in these stories a major theme emerges -- people are not prizes, but beings with their own free will.

The Controller

In films about control, protagonists and antagonists battle for control of someone, some place, or something. Many times the battle is for control of the protagonist's freedom. In *Star Wars: A New Hope*, Luke Skywalker and The Emperor both want to control the fate of the galaxy. In *Mad Max: Fury Road*, the battle is for Max's freedom similar to the battle Andy Dufrane faces in *The Shawshank Redemption* and Maximus faces in *Gladiator.*

In *Cinderella,* she must battle against her evil
Stepmother for control of her life. In *The Dark Knight,*
Batman and the Joker battle for control of Gotham.
In *Jaws,* Chief Brody and the shark battle for control
of the beach. This structure is also the basis for most
horror films, where a protagonist battles against a
supernatural force for control of a physical space or
the character's life.

Whatever your antagonist's desire, it should be as
equally motivated as your protagonist's. The "bad guy"
always has a compelling moral argument in strong
stories. We understand why the character is chasing
after their desire. In the best stories, we see a little of
ourselves in both the protagonist and the antagonist.

SHOW ME THE MAGIC!
3 PRINCIPLES FOR GIVING YOUR CHARACTERS UNUSUAL POWERS

Blake Snyder once referred to a genre of films he dubbed "genie in a bottle" stories. These are films where the protagonist is endowed with some special gifting or ability that they believe will solve all their problems. Of course, in the end the magic usually backfires on the character and reinforces the age-old theme that you can't use shortcuts to solve your problems. Here are three principles to follow if you plan to bestow magic on your main character.

The Magic Should Address A Need You've Already Established For The Character

It's important that the magic you give your character provide a solution for a problem you've spent time establishing as an issue in their life. Certainly, the fun in these stories is watching the character receive and then use the magic, but failing to build a landscape in the first act where the magic is truly useful can be detrimental to the overall arc. In *Shallow Hal*, we are given a front row seat to watch Hal's judgment of others based on physical appearance. The writers waste no time letting us in on what a problem this is for him. When Tony Robbins grants Hal the unusual gift of seeing people physically based on their inner selves, Hal's problem appears to be cured. Of course, things become complex when Hal loses the magic and is forced to appreciate the inner beauty aside from the physical appearance of a woman he has already fallen in love with. In the end, Hal must embrace the beauty inside of someone being superior to all else, which is

where the true magic lies. Jim Carey's character in
Liar Liar faces a similar issue. However, while Hal's
magic makes life enjoyable, Carey's magic turns him
into a lawyer unable to tell a lie – something that jolts
his world upside down. The humor of watching Carey
react to such a predicament only works because we
spend the first act of the story establishing how his
life is structured around his ability to lie so effectively.
Flubber fulfills the deepest desires of Sherman Klump
in *The Nutty Professor*, but only after we've established
that he has some serious social problems resulting
from his weight. It's essential we establish the
character's blind spot before we let a genie appear on
the scene.

The Magic Should Intoxicate Your Character and Rob Them of their Better Judgment

In another role, Jim Carey continues to enchant as
a character endowed with magical abilities in *Bruce
Almighty*. The humor here rises from watching Carey
play God and clumsily grant prayer requests. It's
worth mentioning that the film also contains a crucial
element for making this type of magic work: rules.
When God gives Bruce his powers, he insists on
two things. First, he can't tell anyone he's God. And
second, he can't affect free will. These rules become
important in causing Bruce to make decisions beyond
his good judgment. Even with these limitations,
Bruce becomes drunk with power using his magic
to part a bowl of tomato soup and blow a woman's
skirt up. It quickly becomes clear that the world is
not a better place under Bruce's rule. In *Office Space*,
Peter Gibbons falls into a magic trance that frees him
from the concerns of corporate life. The extent of his

intoxication grows increasingly humorous as Peter eventually ends up fileting a freshly caught fish on his desk at work. The lack of concern quickly becomes a lack of judgment after he rationalizes theft from the company, roping his dear friends into his downward spiral. In the best stories, our protagonist will not only sail their own ship into the abyss, but they take others with them. The closer their relationships with those they entrap, the higher the stakes will become.

The Magic Won't Solve Your Problems and Must Be Given Up

After the protagonist abuses their powers, there's only one solution to return life to normalcy – give up the magic. In stories such as *Bruce Almighty*, the magic must literally be given up. In other tales, the sacrifice is more metaphoric. Drew Barrymore gives up the magic of her perceived youth in *Never Been Kissed* while Dustin Hoffman gives up his magical celebrity status in *Tootsie*. In *E.T.,* the magic of E.T.'s presence must be given up by Elliott. In *Mean Girls*, the magic of popularity must be given up to return to a peaceful life. Even Dorothy must give up Oz to return home. With every example, the theme is the same. Magic won't solve your problems. There is no way around the difficulty, only through it. Shortcuts just don't work when it comes to things that matter. Stories where characters fulfill our own fantasies by taking magical opportunities or abilities out for a test drive touch a place in our psyche that will always itch. There's also a comfort in being reminded that while these fantasies are fun, they won't get us where we need to be. Only hard work can do that – a truth that every committed writer knows well.

HEARING VOICES:
3 TYPES OF VOICE-OVER THAT STRENGTHEN STORIES

The use of voice-over in scriptwriting has been hotly contested for years. Every writer would likely admit it risks confusing the audience when a disembodied voice speaks without context clues as to who's narrating the story in front of us. Some feel voice-over is a lazy method that allows the writer to simply tell the audience what a character is thinking rather than going through the difficult exercise of showing them. Others feel it adds another layer to the story, giving the viewer a chance to experience both the inner world of the character as well as the outer world.

In the film, *Adaptation*, Robert McKee famously shouts, "God help you if you use voice-over in your work, my friends. God help you. That's flaccid, sloppy writing. Any idiot can write a voice-over narration to explain the thoughts of a character." If we're honest, McKee's words ring true the vast majority of the time. Voice-over has a well-deserved reputation because writers who lacked skill have used it so often as a crutch. So, is it EVER appropriate? The revered *Citizen Kane* used voice-over, right? What do we say about filmmakers like Stanley Kubrick who used the method in films ranging from *Barry Lyndon* to Full *Metal Jacket*? Here are three ways that voice-over has been used to strengthen a script instead of diluting its visual power.

Adding Poetic Voice to the Story

Some storytellers have a natural poetry in their voice. Using a poetic voice-over can elevate a script to high art, while using this method prematurely as a writer can leave a bad taste in a reader's mouth. In *Taxi Driver*, the voice of Travis Bickle paints a cultural picture of life in all its loneliness. It causes us to more deeply consider his actions and search for metaphor in the story. We see a similar use of voice-over in *Apocalypse Now*. The voice-over in *A Scanner Darkly* keeps the story faithful to the poetic nature of Phillip K. Dick's writing in the literary work the film is based on. Jack's voice-over in *Fight Club* accomplishes the same purpose. These examples bring us to the next way that voice-over is effectively used – to bring the spirit of a book to its adaptation.

Bringing the Spirit of a Book to Its Adaptation

Many of the most powerful stories to ever hit the big screen began in the pages of a novel or short story. A great number of good stories have had the ability to transcend the medium they were created in and find life in another medium altogether. Screenwriters will often honor the impact of the original work by using voice-over to keep powerful words and passages from the source in play. It could be argued that Red's voice-over in *The Shawshank Redemption* is one of the most memorable in all of film. It transcended the source material and brought perspective to the story that greatly reinforced the themes in Stephen King's original *Rita Hayworth and the Shawshank Redemption*. Gordy's words have a similar effect in *Stand By Me*. The voice-overs in *A Christmas Story* and *Forrest Gump* have become cultural catch phrases enjoyed by generations of film goers. The method has worked in adaptations across genres as well. Voice-overs in *Blade Runner* and *Dune* exemplify their power in Sci-Fi. *A Clockwork Orange* and *American Psycho* exemplify their power in psychological thrillers. Even *Election*, *High Fidelity*, and *The Princess Bride* demonstrate their power in comedies.

Providing the Audience an Objective (Or Non-Objective) View

There are a number of ways to provide the audience a view that balances the story being told. Here are a few of the more common methods.

The Unreliable Narrator

Unreliable narrators are most common in crime stories. They can be used as juxtaposition against what is being seen, demonstrating how skewed the narrator's view might be. This method is used in *Goodfellas*, *Blow*, *Trainspotting* and *Casino*. The narrator can be a voice from beyond the grave, with an agenda about the actions we are seeing on-screen, as in *American Beauty* and *Sunset Boulevard*. They can also be used as a red herring to manipulate the audience into a certain way of thinking as in *The Usual Suspects* and *Psycho*. These kind of narrators add depth to the story, but offer a perspective that is in some way unreliable or non-objective.

The Storybook Narrator

Storybook narrators are meant to be the ultimate voice of objectivity. They have no agenda or "skin in the game." They exist to tell the story. Using this method gives the story a particular feel or framework that does not work for every script. However, when used under the right circumstances, the results are impactful. Alec Baldwin's voice weaves the characters in *The Royal Tenenbaums* together in a way that compliments Wes Anderson's style. Ricky Jay's opening monologue in *Magnolia* sets the stage for a world where frogs will eventually rain from the sky. More recently, Forest Whitaker's voice frames the complex world of *Dope* so that viewers are able to enjoy the characters rather than trying to construct a landscape for the story.

The Jester Narrator

Sometimes the narrator tells us what the character is thinking but cannot say out loud. This is a useful comedic device. It's a method everyone relates to because we've all had thoughts in our head, worthy of a chuckle, that' we'd never actually give voice to. Whether it's Charlie working through his writing process in *Adaptation*, Bridget's reactions to the men in her life in *Bridget Jones's Diary*, or Cher's absurd observations about the world in *Clueless*, comedic voice-over inside the mind of the character can add a great deal to the audience's overall experience.

3 JOURNEYS TO THE UNDERWORLD

Mythologist, Joseph Campbell spoke of the necessity of sending your hero into the underworld. As polite members of society, we often lack the nerve to be as mean to our characters as we might need to be, or want to be. It's in the underworld where our characters will suffer their greatest pain, take on their most profound challenges, and sometimes score their greatest victories. The severity of the underworld can speak to the stakes in the story. The more foreign, dark, and undesirable the underworld seems, the greater emotion the audience experiences when the hero traverses through to safety. Not all underworlds are literal, though some are. Some stories even turn this idea on its head. In *Sling Blade*, Karl Childers ascends *out of the underworld* to fight his toughest battle, only to return *back to the underworld* at the end of the story. Here are three underworlds to send your hero down into.

The Literal Underworld

One of the most classic yet effective scenes in film is when a protagonist descends down a long flight of stairs. This is a sure sign our character is going into the underworld. *The Goonies* descends down a portal in a fireplace to an underworld full of danger and treasure. Clarice Starling descends a dark flight of steps each time she must go visit Hannibal Lecter, who holds the key to what she's looking for in the underworld of *The Silence of the Lambs*. In *Real Genius*, Mitch enters a portal in the closet, taking a mechanical elevator to his underworld. Craig also takes an elevator to the underworld in *Being John*

Malkovich. Clarence must navigate the underworld of
Drexl Spivey in *True Romance.* While Ree must ascend
into the Ozark Mountains to enter the underworld
in *Winter's Bone.* Occasionally the underworld lies
deep inside someone. It might be less literal, but
can be just as harrowing. This is frequently the case
with independent films, but also works with more
general market stories such as *Inside Out,* where the
underworld is literally inside a little girl.

The Underwolrd Of Revolution

The underworld of revolution is seen when a character
descends into a social underground, where coming
change is brewing. In *Suffragette,* Maud goes into
the underground world where people are working
tirelessly to bring about voting rights for women. This
underground is just as dangerous as any a Greek
hero could navigate, full of violence, imprisonment,
and loss. Jackie Robinson must battle in the racist
underworld of Major League Baseball in *42.* Jefferson
Smith does the same in the underworld of politics in
Mr. Smith Goes to Washington. Sometimes the hero
lives to see the world of coming change, as is the
case in *The Social Network,* where Mark Zuckerberg
successfully maneuvers through the underworld of the
tech revolution. Sometimes the hero does not, as is the
case with Ron Woodroof in *Dallas Buyers Club.*

The Underworld Of Another (Sub) Culture

Sending a character into the underworld through a
foreign land is a tried and true method in storytelling,
Bill Murray's hilarious performance in *Rock the
Kasbah* is evidence that this underworld will never

be fully tapped for laughs, chills, or emotional appeal. Tony Mendez takes a similar journey to the underworld of a foreign land in *Argo*. However, sometimes an actual culture change is not appropriate for a story. In these cases, sending a character into a foreign sub-culture can accomplish the same effect. In *Almost Famous*, William Miller descends into the sub-culture of rock and roll. In *Rounders*, Mike McDermott descends into the subculture of high stakes poker, comes out, and then descends right back in, much to the dismay of the audience. In *Whiplash*, Andrew descends into the underworld of classically trained musicians and in *Pitch Perfect*, Beca humorously descends into the underworld of college a cappella. Sub-cultures are endless. The underworlds we can send our characters to are infinite, too.

3 WAYS TO BE GOOD AT BEING BAD:
USING TIME, SPACE, AND UNPLANNED GUESTS TO
BRING CONFLICT TO YOUR STORY

Most writers like to think they're nice people. Is it possible you might be too nice? Have you ever tried to see how mean you can be to your characters? Engaging storytellers quickly learn that becoming diabolical toward their protagonist can be an effective tool for keeping their stories engaging. The ability to increase conflict in a script can be the difference between an audience biting their nails or checking their phone. Most writers have received feedback at some point or another encouraging them to raise the stakes. But, how do you do that? Are there techniques for increasing conflict organically? Here are three ways writers have been good at being bad.

Compressing Time

The least impactful stories seem to drag on forever. There is little in the setup to bring them to conclusion an hour or so later. Some films will literally have a character announce that "it's time to wrap things up and finish this" at the end of the second act. Audiences appreciate when there is a natural element to the story that increases conflict by compressing time. Some have referred to this as the "ticking time bomb" in the story. It's ideal when our protagonist is racing against the clock to accomplish their goal. In *Get Hard*, James King has 30 days before he must report to prison where he will certainly face physical disaster unless Darnell Lewis can help him become street wise before he goes in. As the training continuously goes humorously wrong, we are reminded time and again that the days are slipping by and James will be headed to prison soon whether the duo succeed at their task or not. In Disney's *Cinderella*, it's the Prince who's racing against the clock. He must find true love before he's forced to marry a woman for pure political reasons. Of course, Cinderella is also up against a ticking clock when she arrives at the royal ball. At midnight, everything that has allowed her to be in the palace undetected will disappear, even if she hasn't captured the heart of the prince. When the pace begins to feel slow in your own story, try raising the stakes by giving the protagonist a hard deadline to accomplish their goal.

Compressing Space

The world is a big place. One of the most important jobs a writer has is to keep our protagonist and the antagonistic forces in the story around the same relative area – the closer the better. If the two never have to interact, the stakes, significantly lessen. Horror and suspense films are often masterful at keeping characters in the same space. *The Boy Next Door* wouldn't be very interesting if Claire and Noah lived in different towns. Because he lives next door, suspense is kept alive. Often the protagonist cannot accomplish their goal if they leave the space they're in. Other times, a protagonist and antagonist are competing for the same physical area. In *Jaws*, Brody and the shark both compete for control of the beach. This technique works across genres. In *Jurassic World*, the writers continue to rely on keeping the characters in the same geographic space (the park) with the dinosaurs. Forcing the protagonist into the same competitive arena as the antagonist, or better

yet into the lair of the antagonist, builds tension in the
audience without much additional effort. Forcing them
into a cage where only one can leave is a timeless trope
of good storytelling.

Inviting Unplanned Guests Along

Without question, nothing complicates situations like
people. We all know we need a main character with a
clear goal to create an effective story. We might have
even mastered the use of an antagonist or antagonistic
force to make things more difficult for our hero. But
when we can add additional characters in a natural
way, we create the opportunity to complicate things
even further. In *Unfinished Business*, Dan Trunkman
must travel to Europe to close a deal that will save
him and his family. The goal is clear. But, when
Dan is saddled with the additional baggage of an old
curmudgeon and a quirky, untested rookie, things
get much more complicated and interesting. In *The
Wedding Ringer*, Doug Harris must secure a best man
before his wedding day. Again, we have a clear goal.
But the stakes rise even higher when Doug must also
have convincing groomsmen for the ceremony. Adding
these additional characters gives us more opportunity
for conflict and humor. More than one writer has
benefitted from adding characters to their story mix.
As long as the character serves a purpose and is either
part of helping the protagonist reach their goal or
acting as part of the opposition, they will be a welcome
addition to your script – even if they are unplanned
guests on your protagonist's journey.

LOOK INTO MY EYES:
3 WAYS TO BREAK THE 4TH WALL

For good reason, writers in the early stages of their development are encouraged not to use voiceover in their scripts. One of the key reasons even seasoned writers are weary of doing so is that it breaks the 4th wall between the audience and the performers. However, it's undeniable that some of the most loved and well-written stories break the wall between the viewer and those doing the viewing. Here are a few examples of effective ways to break the 4th wall.

Employ A Storyteller

In Robert Zemeckis's new film, *The Walk*, the protagonist breaks the 4th wall and addresses the audience directly throughout the film, acting as narrator. While remaining a risky move, the device works because we have someone as engaging as Joseph Gordon-Levitt to watch and uncommonly good writing to listen to. Some writers are good at dialogue. Others are wonderful at describing scenes and actions. Still others can use prose in their work to great effect. Few can master all these approaches. While the character in *The Walk* only talks to the audience while on top of the Statue of Liberty, other films feature characters daring to turn to the camera and address us in the middle of a scene. John Cusack's character in *High Fidelity* masterfully and humorously moves between the role of storyteller and protagonist. Uma Thurman opens and closes the *Kill Bill* saga by addressing the audience directly. She remains our storyteller throughout the course of the narrative. Wes Anderson uses unseen storytellers in *The Royal*

Tenenbaums and *The Grand Budapest Hotel.* They break the 4th wall and we never even notice.

Bookend Your Break

Since choosing to break the 4th wall can take your audience out of the experience momentarily, you might choose to use the device sparingly. Films like *American Beauty* use a disembodied narrator only to set up and conclude the action, with perhaps one exception in the middle. Kevin Spacey narrates his world to move us into the story quickly. He lets us know that he is speaking to us from another world. At the end of the second act, he reminds us that he is dead. And finally, wraps up the major themes of the story at the end. Using this bookend approach keeps us from constantly interrupting the narrative by breaking the 4th wall.

Disguise The Break

In *Bruce Almighty*, the writers cleverly created the protagonist as a TV news reporter so that he could look at and address the audience directly from time to time. At the end of the film, he further breaks the 4th wall by giving the film audience a wink and speaking directly to us. Disguising the break also allowed Steve Carell's character to look directly into our eyes while he delivers a hilariously memorable breakdown. *Breaking Bad* uses a similar technique for dramatic effect in it's pilot, allowing Bryan Cranston to look directly into a camera and address those he loves. This puts us in the position of Walter White's family, though we haven't met them yet. We feel deep empathy as the character seems to be talking right at us. Reese Witherspoon and Matthew Broderick rotate back and forth as storytellers in *Election*. They will often pause the action to fill us in on the backstory of the moment we are witnessing. Their tour through the minds of the characters and their backstories actually makes our narrative journey more colorful, rather than taking us out of the story – a perfect disguise. Kevin Smith actually has the characters involved in the backstory address the audience in small vignettes in *Chasing Amy*. The audience becomes pseudo-documentary filmmakers interviewing these subjects about what they know the characters have done previously in their lives.

As with most advanced techniques, breaking the 4th wall usually only works when used sparingly or as a major device in the story. There's not much middle ground in this arena. Addressing the audience directly can powerfully draw them into the story. It can also alienate them and make your story feel less than cinematic. Watch what's worked in the stories you love. Then, go out and out your own creative spin on it.

IN DEFENSE OF DIFFICULT PEOPLE: 3 WAYS TO BUILD EMPATHY FOR DIFFICULT PROTAGONISTS

For some time now, there's been a growing trend among popular protagonists. The new 'Golden Age' of television that we find ourselves in has been built around men and women that most of us would find difficult in real life. Perhaps these characters work because they embody the complexity and conflicted world we find ourselves in. Others have suggested that its simply a matter of showing something we haven't seen in visual stories before. Whatever the case, difficult people have experienced a renaissance on screens, both big and small. The secret behind executing these sorts of protagonists is finding a way to still build empathy for them in the minds and hearts of the audience. Here are three methods you might consider for pulling off such a feat.

Give Them A Soft Spot

In *Save the Cat*, Blake Snyder suggested that audiences will always fall for a character that is nice to children, animals, or the elderly. Regardless of what you think of his 15 beats, Snyder nailed this concept. Audiences have been intrigued by the kind-hearted fiend ever since we first saw Frankenstein's monster pick flowers with a little girl beside a lake. In *Kill Bill: Volume 1*, The Bride refuses to seek her revenge on Vernita Green until her antagonist's daughter is out of harms way. Cold-hearted Gemma Teller Morrow's Achilles heel is her son, Jax, in *Sons of Anarchy*. Even twisted psycho, Garland 'The Marietta Mangler' Greene resists his darker nature thanks to a little girl on her swing set in *Con Air*. The reason a soft spot in the heart of a difficult protagonist works is that it reminds us of their humanity. We've all done regrettable things. When we see characters, who have committed worse travesties than we ever will, manage to locate *their* humanity, we find hope for ourselves as well.

Give Them A Cause

Passion is a tough thing to resist, even in those who do despicable things. Its why talented artists, whose personal lives are problematic, continue to receive the love and support of fans around the world. Film and TV have given us powerful stories about killers who care about the less fortunate, wiseguys who care about the neighborhood, abusive narcissists who care about music, and power-hungry politicians who actually care about the truth. Frank Lucas passes out turkeys to the poor at Thanksgiving in *American Gangster*. Miles Davis gives nothing short of his soul for his music in *Miles Ahead*. Furiosa risks life and limb for the freedom of others in *Mad Max: Fury Road*. Rust Cole alienates everyone around him and wears his darkness on his sleeve, all in a desperate pursuit for truth in *True Detective*. None of these characters would be considered 'nice people' in real life. They all have difficulty dealing with others. They are all tremendously flawed and yet they all still gained a great deal of empathy from their audiences.

Give Them Someone They Can Defend

Bullies are a tough sell as protagonists in the world of story. It's hard for us to feel empathetic towards those who prey on people weaker than themselves. We

only swallow such bitter pills if we can understand
the reason behind such actions – childhood abuse,
insecurity, or perhaps loneliness. While we might not
excuse the character's actions, we will at least have
a greater degree of understanding. We will, however,
overlook even the vilest deeds a character commits
if we see them defend or care for someone weaker
than them. Seeing a difficult character care for a
friend, a little brother, a parent or even an uncle often
softens our feelings about their actions and builds our
empathy.

Larry Flynt takes care of his brother and his wife, even
when they don't deserve it in *The People Vs. Larry
Flynt*. Seeing this causes us to feel more tolerance
towards the lesser appealing parts of his character.
Tony Soprano cares deeply for his son and doesn't
want to see him end up as a gangster, because he's
afraid the boy is too sensitive, in *The Sopranos*. Avon
Barksdale cares for an incapacitated uncle in *The
Wire*, making us feel differently about who he is and
why he does what he does. The trope works in the
comedy genre as well. Ricky Bobby cares deeply about
his shiftless father and defends him mercilessly in
Talladega Nights.

We don't have to agree with everything a protagonist
does. We don't even have to necessarily like them.
However, we do need to feel like we understand them.
Some small part of us must give them the benefit of
the doubt. Working with and even caring about people
who are difficult to deal with is part of life. When we
can demonstrate these people in nuanced ways, we
honor a wider spectrum of humankind. We also then
offer a more authentic version of truth in our stories.

THE MULTI-HEADED BEAST:
THREE WAYS TO TAME A STORY WITH MORE THAN ONE PROTAGONIST

At some point in their career, many writers will decide to work outside the traditional method of telling a story about a single protagonist on a journey. This can be a recipe for disaster and turn into a wild monster that gets away from the writer, causing them to chase their stories down a rabbit hole, often losing their audience somewhere along the way. Here are three ways to tame stories of this sort before they escape from you.

A Team With The Same Goal

One of the simplest approaches to a multi-protagonist story is to create a "team" with the same goal. Even in these "team-based" stories, you may find a single character standing out more than the others. It could be because they are funnier than the others, or have better dialogue, or simply that they have more screen time. However, if we are going to follow a group of people and avoid confusion, the most efficient method will be to give all the protagonistic characters the same goal. In *The Hangover*, all the main characters are searching for their lost friend, Doug. While having the SAME goal, all the character's personalities are DIFFERENT. The same is true in *Bridesmaids*, *Armageddon*, and *Tropic Thunder*. This is key in taming this sort of story – same goal, different personalities. The same approach is often used in sports films where the team's goal is winning (*Friday Night Lights*), space films about astronauts (*The Right Stuff*), and heist films (*Ocean's Eleven*). Television uses the same approach with ensemble casts. In *Orange*

Is The New Black, all of the characters have the
same goal – surviving another day in prison. In *True
Detective*, the crime investigators all want to catch the
killer.

Two Heads Are Better Than One

Sometimes, there are only two characters who could
be considered the protagonist. "Buddy Films" have
been a staple of storytelling for centuries. Many
times, in these sorts of stories, both characters do
share the same goal (*Superbad, Butch Cassidy and
the Sundance Kid, Natural Born Killers and Good
Will Hunting*). However, one character will usually
experience a greater arc (*Thelma and Louise*), but not
always (*Changing Lanes*). Other times, one character
will act as the protagonist and the other will serve as
the main character in the story. We see this in *The
Shawshank Redemption*, where Morgan Freeman is
the protagonist and Tim Robbins is the main character
as well as in *The Sixth Sense*, where Bruce Willis is
the protagonist but Haley Joel Osment is the main
character. Of course, the most common stories that
use dual protagonists are romantic comedies. When
we look closely, these stories are structured nearly
identical to "buddy films." The opposite holds true as
well. While *Hot Pursuit* is not a romantic comedy per
se, this "buddy film" is structured exactly like one.

Multiple Intersecting Stories

This discussion comes with a warning. These stories
are some of the hardest to write and are usually only
successful in the hands of the most gifted storytellers.
They define the domain of advanced and experienced

writers. Storytellers should work to earn the right
to tell these types of stories. Robert Altman is likely
the best-known master of the multi-narrative film.
Nashville, Short Cuts, and *A Prairie Home Companion*
are all testaments to the power these stories can have.
Anyone wishing to work in narratives of this sort
should begin with Altman. Both Wes Anderson and
Paul Thomas Anderson have done excellent work with
ensemble casts. *The Royal Tenenbaums* and *Magnolia*
certainly demonstrate that both writers understand
how to execute multiple intersecting stories well. The
key to all the above mentioned films is that at least one
character have a clear journey with a marked external
goal. They do not necessarily have to be the character
with the most screen time, but having this element will
create a more organic space for the other characters to
breathe and function in.

Critics are divided on ensemble stories such as
Crash, State and Main, and *Love Actually.* Yet, all
found deeply connect and devoted to audiences. This
method has been successful in a wide range of genres
including comic book adaptations (*Sin City* and *The
Avengers*), independent faire (*Little Miss Sunshine* and
I Heart Huckabees), and even action films (*Smoking
Aces* and *The Expendables*). Those serious about
attempting this form of storytelling might also want to
take a look at *Grand Hotel, Diner, Best In Show, Death
At A Funeral* and *Babel.*

WHAT'S IT ALL ABOUT?
4 CATEGORIES OF THEMES FOR CONSTRUCTING STORIES

All too often, storytellers deal with the themes in their stories as an afterthought. It's unfortunate when we fail to realize that the theme is actually what the story is about. It's the wise lesson of truth that our hero must learn over the course of the story. It's easy to confuse the theme with the external goal. Sometimes storytellers will say a character's external goal is to "learn" or "realize" something. But we can't quite *see* someone learn or realize anything. When our hero learns and/or realizes something, we are in the domain of the theme, not the external goal. The theme also embodies what the storyteller has to say to the world (and often about the world) through narrative. The theme should be something to which the writer has personal connection.

There's a common old adage that tells writers to write what they know. Many mistakenly believe this means that if you haven't lived in space, drawn a gun in the old west, or walked in the shoes of a gangster, you shouldn't write about it. The saying isn't meant to apply to the details or setting of the story, it's meant to apply to the theme. Write the THEMES that you know. Write the truths that you have experienced. Write what you KNOW to be true. While the theme should come across through the action of the characters, it's sometimes directly spoken by a secondary character to the hero early on in the story -- when the line of dialogue seems unimportant. It risks being on the nose, but occasionally a character will state directly what they learned – and thus the theme - as Dorothy does in *The Wizard of Oz*, when she declares, "There's no place like home." Here are four categories of themes to consider when constructing your story.

Addition By Subtraction

The biggest gains in life sometimes come through the experience of loss or giving something up. This is a hard lesson that almost every human being experiences at some point in his or her life. It's no wonder it remains such a popular theme in stories. In *Southpaw*, Billy Hope learns that acting on everything you feel will cause immeasurable tragedy in your life that takes months, if not years, to repair, if it can be repaired at all. He only learns this through the tragic loss of his wife and daughter. Joy learns that we need *all* our emotions to be healthy, not just the ones that make us feel good, in *Inside Out*. She must give up control in order to fully grasp this truth. Films like *Bruce Almighty*, *Liar Liar*, and *Shallow Hal* demonstrate that you can't use magic to solve your problems, either. You must give up the magic and solve problems by dealing with them head on if you want to succeed. In *Paper Towns*, our protagonist comes to realize the biggest miracle in life is not a special person, place, or event. It's the journey we take to get to these people, places, and events. *Me and Earl and the Dying Girl* backs the same theme.

It Takes A Village

We can't do it alone. It's a lesson so many people never learn. We need each other. We will always be capable of so much more when we combine our forces than we ever were flying solo. This theme plays out in a great number of sports movies, as it could be argued that this theme is actually the point of all team sports. We see it in *Hoosiers* when the team realizes they need more than their superstar, Jimmy, to go the distance. *Friday Night Lights*, *Remember the Titans*, and *We are Marshall* also play out this theme. This theme often finds its way out of the sports genre also. In *Mr. Holmes*, Sherlock Holmes learns just how much he needs his housekeeper and her son. And in the comedy classic, *Funny Farm*, Chevy Chase and his wife learn how much they need the townspeople they had come to hate.

Don't Count Me Out

An old prophesy sates a child shall lead them. Sometimes that child is not a physical child, but a mental child or even a child in their maturity. Sometimes this theme reinforces the joy we experience in watching "the court jester" act as king. Other times, showing the unexpected victory of the underdog or fish out of water reinforces the theme. In *Dope*, the victors are the kids at school that everyone thinks are weird. In *Forrest Gump*, *Napoleon Dynamite*, and *Bean*, the fool turns out to be not so foolish after all. Storytellers owe it to themselves to watch Peter Sellers master this sort of story in *Being There*. His *Pink Panther* films always reinforce this theme as well. More recently, we've seen *Paul Blart: Mall Cop* attempt to pick up this mantle and reinforce this popular theme. In many of these stories, our hero is not a fool at all, but an underestimated underdog. We see this in *Finding Forrester* and *The Devil Wears Prada*. Occasionally, it's a literal child who leads others to success. Elliot brings his family together; despite being the least likely in *E.T.* Sean Astin accomplishes this in both *Rudy* and *The Goonies*. And in *Big*, a child is responsible for great successes, even though he inhabits the body of a grown man.

Love Wins

This theme communicates one simple idea - love conquers any obstacle in its path. Richard Gere's love overcomes the fact that Julia Roberts is a prostitute in *Pretty Woman*. Ben Stiller's love overcomes time, distance, and embarrassment to unite with Cameron Diaz in *There's Something About Mary*. In *Knocked Up*, Seth Rogen and Katherine Heigel overcome unplanned pregnancy to find love. Eddie Murphy overcomes the trappings of his riches to find love with an average woman in *Coming To America*. Hugh Grant overcomes the trappings of being average to find love with a rich, famous woman in *Notting Hill*. The greater the obstacle or sacrifice in your story, the more enchanting the theme becomes when your characters make their sacrifices and learn their lessons -- all in the pursuit of true love.

PULLING THE PLUG:
4 EMOTIONAL ENDINGS FOR YOUR STORY

Stories are usually built around two journeys. There's an external journey and the internal journey. The former encompasses the *plot points* of the story. In this journey, the protagonist has a clear photographable goal. They are searching for someone, some place, or some thing. When they achieve the goal, the audience has no doubt that the story is complete. In the internal journey, the protagonist is growing and developing. It's in this journey that we see the *character arc*. The character learns something. They overcome something within themselves. They often face their fears or rid themselves of the crutch that's been helping them get by. Internally, a protagonist has a dramatic desire or "want" of which they're keenly aware of and in pursuit of. They also have a dramatic need of which they're often unaware. The relationship between these internal processes builds to give us the emotional ending of the story. Here are four endings to consider for your protagonist.

Positive Ending:
The Protagonist Gets What They Want
And What They Need

This ending is the ultimate "happily ever after." The protagonist finds the treasure and gets the love of the girl. This is usually the sort of ending we see in Disney films and most children's movies. However, the ending can also be found in almost every other genre. In *Argo*, Ben Affleck's character gets the hostages safely out of Iran and is able to re-connect with his family. Dwayne Johnson's character has a similar arc in *San*

Andreas. In *Pretty Woman,* Richard Gere's character gets the girl and saves an old man's company, proving he's changed both internally and externally. In *Back to the Future,* Michael J. Fox's Marty McFly is able to reconstruct the family he needs and get back home.

Negative Irony Ending:
The Protagonist Gets What They Want
But Not What They Need

The ironic part of a negative irony ending is that the protagonist gets one thing but not the other. In *The Social Network,* Jesse Eisenberg's Mark Zuckerberg creates the ultimate social network, but ironically loses all his friends in the process. Liam Neeson's Oskar Schindler saves thousands of Jews from death in *Schindler's List* but ironically implodes in the film's conclusion over his own perceived selfishness. Sean Penn's character gets revenge for his daughter's murder in *Mystic River* but ironically is left more disturbed. In *Presumed Innocent,* Harrison Ford's character is found innocent of the murder he is accused of but is ironically left to serve out a different sort of life sentence when he discovers (spoiler!) that his wife is actually the murderer. Kevin Spacey gains the freedom he longs for in *American Beauty* but loses the family (and life) he's taken for granted in the process. Tom Hanks has a similar experience in *Castaway.*

Positive Irony Ending:
The Protagonist Gets What They Need
But Not What They Want

Though the protagonist doesn't get what they want with these types of endings, they still leave the audience happy and fulfilled. They reinforce the lesson that what we need is often more significant than what we want. Sylvester Stallone loses the match in *Rocky*, but gets the love he needs and proves to himself he can go the distance. Joy doesn't get to control everything in *Inside Out*, but discovers that a healthy person needs all their emotions to achieve happiness. Elliot doesn't get to keep his new father figure in *E.T.* But in helping him return home, his family has somehow been put back together. In *Forrest Gump*, Tom Hanks loses the person he pursues the entire film, Jenny, but gains the love and family he needs through their son. Even Indiana Jones gives up the Holy Grail in *Indiana Jones and the Last Crusade*, in order to have the approval of his father – the thing he actually needs most.

Negative Ending:
The Protagonist Gets Neither What They Want
Nor What They Need

These endings are the most difficult to pull off. American audiences don't often respond to stories where characters get neither what they want nor what they need. Endings of this sort are usually reserved for R-rated dramas. However, from time to time, we do see this ending masterfully executed, usually by a master storyteller. In *Up in the Air*, George Clooney gets neither what he wants nor what he needs. Jack

Nicholson's R.P. McMurphy gains neither his freedom nor understanding of who he is in *One Flew Over the Cuckoo's Nest*. Johnny Depp experiences a similar arc in *Blow*. Leonardo DiCaprio loses everything he gains including the respect and love of his family in *The Wolf of Wall Street*. And while technically the first part in a longer story, as a standalone film, Ana Steele gets neither what she wants nor what she needs in *Fifty Shades of Grey*.

4 HORROR ARCHETYPES THAT WORK IN ANY GENRE

Unless you work in the genre, screenwriters often ignore horror films. This can be to our own demise, as there are many powerful themes, tropes, and archetypes used that transcend stories of horror and suspense. Here are some of the archetypes found in horror scripts that can be used in any genre.

The Ghost

Screenwriting gurus have long recommended having a "ghost" that haunts your protagonist. The "ghost" is a person or event in the protagonist's past that still causes them trouble. Sometimes, this will be a very external experience for your character, such as when a person from their past shows up unexpectedly. The look on Viggo Mortensen's face is unforgettable when shady figures from his past emerge to haunt his present circumstances in *A History of Violence*. An unexpected sexual tryst with James Marsden haunts Jack Black's character in the recently released *The D Train*. Other times, the "ghost" only haunts the protagonist internally. We are only aware of their presence through a brief flashback or line of dialogue. Ray Charles's character in *Ray* is plagued with guilt throughout the film by the childhood death of his brother. *Saving Mr. Banks, Stand By Me, Ordinary People, Patch Adams,* and *Good Will Hunting* all utilize this archetype in their stories.

The Monster

An excellent way to maintain ongoing conflict in your story is to create a "monster" that the protagonist must occasionally battle, be hunted by, or run from. Monsters in stories can take on many forms and don't necessarily serve as the antagonist in the script. The shark is the "monster" in *Jaws,* but not the true antagonist. God serves as the "monster" in *Time Bandits.* In *Birdman,* the character by the same name serves as both a "monster" and a "ghost," plaguing Michael Keaton. While there is a specific character serving as the antagonist in *Selma,* the police act collectively as a "monster" facing down MLK.

The Vampire

A vampire is a character that sucks the life force or potential from the protagonist – sometimes in a malicious fashion and sometimes unintentionally. They might be the good-natured friends that keep our main character from being all they can be – as in *Good Will Hunting.* Or they might be the husband sucking his wife's talent and taking credit for her work – as in *Big Eyes.* Kathy Bates plays a classic "vampire" to Adam Sandler's Bobby Boucher in *The Waterboy.* In *Cinderella,* the protagonist's stepmother and wicked stepsisters continually suck life and opportunity away from her. In most cases, our main character must either stand up to the "vampire" or flee from them by the story's end.

The Frankenstein

Frankenstein was, of course, known for striking fear in the hearts of those around him, but actually not being innately harmful at all. In a classic scene from cinema, we remember a little girl with a flower tames this "savage beast." In *To Kill A Mockingbird*, Boo Radley is a "Frankenstein" that everyone in the neighborhood is afraid of. In the end, he rescues Scout from harm is known as a protector of those around him. The point of the "Frankenstein" archetype is to reveal shortcomings in the protagonist or the society they live in, not shortcomings in the "Frankenstein." We see that our main character actually had no reason to be afraid and we are reminded that there are people and things in our own lives that we live in fear of – without good reason.

We see "Frankesnteins" in *The Wizard of Oz* (The Cowardly Lion and The Wizard), *The Goonies* (Sloth), and *Sling Blade* (Karl Childers). We even see a subtle version of this "Frankenstein" scenario in *Ex Machina* in the interaction between Caleb and Ava. In many stories, the "Frankenstein" will either have their true nature revealed, be destroyed by those who live in fear of them, or become the destroyer themselves.

MARCH MADNESS:
THE FINAL FOUR LESSONS OF
BASKETBALL STORIES

For some people, March means only one thing – basketball. Even if you're not a sports fan, it's likely you've seen at least one film that uses basketball as a backdrop for its plot. Sports stories are easy to structure. They inherently contain the necessary elements for a good narrative. We have one team or player we are rooting for. We have another that we want to see lose. The stakes and the external goal are clear. There is that built-in ticking clock, counting the minutes away as we race towards a victor. Here are four lessons we can take from some of the best basketball stories ever crafted.

COACH CARTER
It's Not About the Players

In many ways, basketball is a lot like filmmaking. They are both team activities. One person can't do everything. It takes cooperation and sacrifice to have a winning product in the end. On the highest level, both require a talented leader. A basketball coach will not be shooting the ball at the final buzzer, but he or she will be guiding the player that does. A director will not be stepping in front of the camera to act out a scene, except in the rare case of the director/actor, but they will guide the actor that does. Throughout sports history, we've learned that the story of the coach is often just as compelling as the stories of the players. While it might be difficult to choose a single player to focus on when crafting a story, focusing on the coach might be an easier and more emotionally resonant solution. In *Coach Carter*, Samuel L. Jackson's character teaches his players that there are things in life more important than winning. His responsibility to mold the character of the team outweighs his responsibility to mold their skills on the court. And because of his willingness to sacrifice, we love him and root for his team.

WHITE MEN CAN'T JUMP
It's Not About the Fame

Not all great basketball stories take place inside school gymnasiums or sports arenas. Basketball takes on a completely different philosophy when played on asphalt. Pick-up games in city parks are a high-stakes environment where some players make their living and reputation on the courts. Stadiums will never fill to watch these players and they will likely never receive an endorsement deal from Nike, but the seriousness with which games are played can rival any college or NBA event. In *White Men Can't Jump*, we see cruel lessons about honor among thieves. Woody Harrelson hustles unsuspecting players for money, until he gets hustled by Wesley Snipes. They soon discover they can combine their skills to pull off the ultimate hustle. However, the duo soon is out-hustled by another group of hustlers. Their only chance of saving the things that matter to them most is to play the game straight up. They must decide, is it the game they love or the hustle? Forcing characters into situations where they must choose between two appealing or unappealing options is one of the best ways to show what they are made of.

HOOSIERS
It's Not About the Coach

There are places in America where life actually revolves around basketball. Players are made to be gods. Coaches can be revered as holy or despised as traitors. Some basketball stories brilliantly demonstrate how the game should never be about any individual player, but also shouldn't be about the coach. Showing that the collective is more important than the singular can be a difficult thing to do when writing a script, as cinematic structure often lends its self to celebrating the accomplishments of one individual more than the rest. *Hoosiers* makes this point when Gene Hackman's character intentionally gets himself thrown out of a game in order to let an assistant coach rise to the occasion. One theme that will always resonate with an audience is when one person sacrifices for the greater good of the group. *Hoosiers* proves to be a masterpiece at establishing this idea.

HE GOT GAME
It's Not About the Game

The best basketball stories are not really about basketball at all. They might use the sport as an environment for the hero to succeed or fail. They might even use winning as an external goal for the protagonist and include that final shot from the half-court line just as the buzzer sounds. However, at the end of the day, we want to know that the hero cares about something more. We want to know that their priorities include the things in life that really matter – family, friends, love, happiness. One of the most effective ways to do this is to pull the hero's family or love interest into the picture. We don't need much setup to understand that someone cares for their family. *He Got Game* is about one of the tightest family relationships, that between parent and child, specifically between father and son. The story centers around how difficult finding our path in life can be without someone we trust to guide us. The bottom line for basketball stories mirrors the bottom line for all other stories. Audiences need to care about the characters whether or not they care about their professions or hobbies. There are a great number of people who don't watch sports on television but will go see a movie about a sports team. This is because intrinsically, we understand that sports are metaphors for life. There are winners. There are losers. There are champions and there are underdogs. If we see a player or a team come from behind to win the big game, deep down, we believe that just might be possible for us too.

ANALYZING THE JUICE: 4 STORY LESSONS FROM AMERICAN CRIME STORY: THE PEOPLE VS. OJ SIMPSON

Many people have been astonished by the success of *The People vs. OJ Simpson*. However, the quality of the writing and the show in general has been no surprise to those familiar with the work of its creators, Scott Alexander and Larry Karaszewski. The duo has made a career out of examining the lives of men they believed to be misunderstood, but deemed evil by some. Ed Wood, Andy Kauffman, and Larry Flynt are just a few of the people they have brought to the silver screen with their stories before tackling Simpson. As with their other work, this nuanced, complex, and layered, story containts secrets that can be seen once we begin digging into the show. Here are four story lessons from *American Crime Story: The People vs. OJ Simpson*.

Lesson #1
Supporting Characters Can Make Or Break The Story

Obviously, *The People vs. OJ* has a basis in real events. Not only is the show based around the book by Jeffrey Toobin, the characters and events in the story actually existed – fairly recently. Since Simpson's trial was very public, even the most minor characters involved became house hold names. The creators of the show, in order to do justice to the story, were faced with the task of creating a large ensemble cast, all of whom needed to have their own differentiating characteristics and personalities. While some of the characters were interesting personas in real life, all were not. The creators had to pick and choose which supporting characters were necessary to the story, which would create the most conflict, and which would most securely hold the audience's attention. Because the supporting characters were so brilliantly captured on the page, acting talent came out of the woodwork in order to portray these iconic characters. In many ways, the supporting characters are what give the show its captivating texture. The creators have succeeded in making us feel as much empathy for many of the supporting players as we do the leading cast.

Lesson #2
Details Matter

With such an epic story, it would have been easy for the writers of the show to stick to the broad strokes. The more difficult route would be to make judgment calls about what moments in the story should be focused on, and then go deep in the details. Fortunately, the writers chose the latter. In many ways, the details in the Simpson case are what the lawyers used to get Simpson acquitted. If jurors had only focused on the broad strokes, it's likely Simpson would have been found guilty. The writers recognized this fact and made highlighting details a theme of the show. Did it matter to jurors that Simpson had a large picture of him and his mother in his home? Who knows? But that simple detail tells us volumes about who Johnnie Cochran was and how he approached defending his client. It's always the details that reveal the most about the characters.

Lesson #3
Some Characters Need Dimension
But Some Characters Should Be Flat

One of the most intriguing episodes of the season is *Marcia, Marcia, Marcia*. Building out Marcia Clark as a fully realized, multi-dimensional character has made the story compelling. The public did not get to see this side of Clark on television, so we feel we are getting an inside view of a person we all thought we knew. We needed to understand the layers that make up Marcia Clark in order to engage in the battle she faces inside the courtroom. Certainty, Lance Ito is just as complex a person in real life. However, for the purposes of the story, his character needed to be flat. We only get a few minor details about him that inform the role he serves in this story. The writers masterfully chose which characters to (and not to!) dissect.

Lesson #4
Even If We Know How A Story Ends,
It's The Journey That Matters

There is likely not one single viewer watching *The People vs. OJ Simpson* that isn't aware that OJ is eventually found not guilty in his criminal trial. However, in that moment on the show, my guess is the writers will still manage to have us on the edge of our seats waiting for the verdict. This is the power of good storytelling. This is why we can watch a movie again and again and become invested emotionally with each viewing. The point of the show is not to reveal Simpson's innocence or guilt. The point of the show is the journey – the human drama of watching all these characters move toward the same finish line. We know that Clark and Darden lose the case, but we might not understand *why*. We know that Simpson walks out of that courtroom a free man, but understanding *why* that happens is why we watch the show. One of the most difficult things to execute in a script is not how the plot unfolds, but why it happens this way. We seek the thrill of the external journey, but it is the internal journey of the characters—primary and secondary— that causes us to remember and revere films and television shows.

ON THE ROAD:
4 ROADS YOUR PROTAGONIST CAN TAKE IN A ROAD MOVIE

Year after year, we see the resurgence of the road movie. We're traveling *Fury Road* with *Mad Max*. We're hitting the open road and heading back to Wally World in *Vacation*. Even ladies like Reese Witherspoon and Sofia Vergara have taken to the road in *Hot Pursuit*. Road movies have long been popular with audiences perhaps because their design usually gives our main characters a clear external goal as well as a path for getting there. Here are four popular roads that writers have utilized in crafting their stories.

THE CROOKED ROAD:
Wild twists & turns to get to an absurd destination

Whether it's Pee Wee Herman hitting the road to retrieve his stolen bicycle from the basement of the Alamo, or Harold and Kumar facing down all that lies between them and a White Castle hamburger, a protagonist whose path leads through the craziest parts of town, past the most colorful characters keeps audiences guessing at what might be around the next curve. A key to these types of stories is in the absurd nature of what lies at the end of the road. In *Little Miss Sunshine*, a pageant for little girls awaits at the destination. In *National Lampoon's Vacation*, it's Wally World. Often times, it's what the character will then attempt to execute once they reach the destination that's important. In *Fanboys*, the protagonist will try to break in to Skywalker Ranch in order to help his friend see the first *Star Wars* prequel before he dies. In *Borat*, our main character will propose to Pamela Anderson when he reaches Hollywood. And in *Road Trip*, Travis will attempt to stop a sex tape from reaching his girlfriend. Other times, the task will be mundane. Harry and Lloyd simply want to return a brief case when they reach their destination of Aspen, Colorado, in *Dumb and Dumber*.

THE STRAIGHT ROAD:
The Inner Journey

Sometimes, the road our protagonist takes has no twists and turns at all – at least externally. These stories focus on the inner journey our character takes while getting to a destination. In *Broken Flowers* Bill Murray attempts to track down four former lovers to meet his son. In Spike Lee's *Get on the Bus*, the men simply all are journeying to The Million Man March. However, a great deal of growth and development occurs on that bus trip. In *Nebraska*, a man and his son travel to the city of Lincoln to collect a million dollar prize, despite the fact the son knows no prize awaits them. The journey their relationship takes is the real story of the film. In *Stand By Me*, four boys journey to see a dead body – but discover what it means to truly live along the way. In these stories, the inner road is always the bumpiest and filled with the most danger. The stakes are often emotional and require the use of metaphor in order to give external signs of what is occurring on the character's interior.

THE ROAD TO NOWHERE:
Just trying to get away

Sometimes, our protagonist only has one place they
are trying to get – away. Escape films have keep people
on the edge of their seats for decades. In *Mad Max:
Fury Road*, Max is simply trying to escape his captors.
Getting to the "green place" is secondary to his desire
just to outrun his enemies. We see the same road used
in films like *Bonnie and Clyde*. Cheryl Strayed is trying
to escape her own demons in *Wild* by hitting the open
trail. Jack Nicholson and Peter Fonda are heading
towards nothing but perhaps a spiritual awakening in
Easy Rider. Road films like *Chicken Run* offer a more
humorous take on escape. And *Ferris Bueller's Day Off*
is a road movie where all our protagonist escapes is
responsibility.

THE CIRCULAR ROAD:
To get back home

Some of the finest road movies are about characters
simply trying to get back home. *Homeward Bound: The
Incredible Journey* and *E.T.* are clear examples. We see
the same road in *Madagascar*, *The Warriors*, and *The
Adventures of Milo and Otis*. Chris Farley and David
Spade hit the road in *Tommy Boy* to save the family
business. Marty McFly travels through time to get
back home in *Back to the Future*. And no discussion of
road movies about returning home is complete without
mentioning *O Brother, Where Art Thou?* Perhaps the
most memorable road movie of all time is *The Wizard
of Oz*. Dorothy befriends fascinating characters,
escapes death-defying dangers, and completes a
gauntlet of challenges just to get back home. The

lesson of this story echoes one of the most common themes used in road movies – there's simply no place like home.

4 STRENGTHS OF THE FEMALE PROTAGONIST

It's no secret that women's voices have been historically underrepresented in the world of film and storytelling in general. Newer movies such as *Suffragette* will continue to expand the body of films that tell stories of strong women. However, smart writers have long realized the power a female protagonist holds. Here are four unique opportunities these characters bring to a story.

The Opportunity for Rare Stories to Now Be Told

There are certain perspectives only women will have. Stories of mothers, daughters, grandmothers, aunts and sisters have been mysteriously absent from the historical archives of narrative. There remains a wealth of untapped experience in the human condition that scriptwriters have avoided, mistakenly assuming that audiences wouldn't show up for, or been simply unaware of. The stories of women in middle passages of life are finding a greater presence on the screen. This year alone, *Rikki and the Flash* attracted the mammoth talents of Meryl Streep as well as a faithful audience and Lily Tomlin brought a story we had never experienced before to life in *Grandma. Wild* could not have packed the power it did with a male protagonist. Cheryl Strayed's story resonated with audiences BECAUSE she was a woman on this journey not in spite of this fact.

The Opportunity for Twice as Many Antagonists

Audiences have been less likely to respond to stories where a male protagonist battles it out against a

woman. We could examine reasons why this might
be the case. Or we can simply recognize the fact that
female protagonists can face off against males *and*
females *and* still delight audiences. *The Hunger Games*
franchise has demonstrated this with dramatic box
office numbers as has the *Divergent* series. Angelina
Jolie has single handedly removed any doubt about
the potential success of matching a woman against
any antagonist in *Tombraider*, *Salt*, and several others.
Kill Bill Vol. 1 and 2, *Sucker Punch*, and *Lucy* have all
found success with audiences and demonstrated the
wide variety of antagonists a female protagonist is
capable of dealing with.

The Opportunity That Exists Because Fewer Stories Of Women's Experiences Have Been Told

As writers, we're often reminded that there's really
nothing new. Everything has been done. It will only
be a matter of how we remix it. It's important to
remember, however, that the catalogue of women's
stories is a much smaller tome than that of men's. We
have seen the story of an American cowboy taming the
Wild West a million times, but we have yet to see the
story of a woman in that environment that resonates
with audiences and finds box office success. The
untapped possibilities are truly endless. We had never
experienced what it was like to be a woman working
in a youth care facility until *Short Term 12*. Beyond
the exploitation films, we had never journeyed with a
woman serving out a prison sentence until *Orange is
the New Black*. We've seen women run drug rings in
Weeds. Women come of age in *Diary of A Teenage Girl*.
And a woman try to raise a son while kidnapped in
Room. And still it feels as though women's stories are

only beginning to be told.

The Opportunity To Challenge Cultural Norms

Many writers are looking for opportunities to tell stories that make a difference – stories that will comfort the disturbed and disturb the comfortable. There is perhaps no greater opportunity to do this than through a female protagonist. From the early days of film, this has been a winning approach. In the late 1930s, the norm was men going on adventures. However, none were as endearing as the young woman who ventured from Kansas to the land of Oz. Challenging what was popular and accepted brought generation after generation to the theater to journey with Dorothy as she traversed wicked antagonists and found friendship along the way. The same could be said of Alice in *Alice in Wonderland*. Currently Julianne Moore and Ellen Page are challenging cultural norms in *Freeheld*. Emily Blunt is challenging a completely different norm in *Sicario*. And Claire Daines has continued to challenge the norms of what women were supposed to do in *Homeland*. This is to say nothing of women born in bodies they don't identify with. *Transparent* has demonstrated that challenging cultural norms can resonate with audiences and make the story a critical darling.

It would be remiss not to address the subject of males writing stories with female protagonists. Certainly, women write stories of men on a daily basis that feel authentic and truthful. However, we have had thousands of years of storytelling from the male perspective. Everyone is fairly familiar with that lens. Men can certainly be capable of writing authentic

female protagonists. However, it's important to do a
bit of extra homework, so that the character is not the
portrayal of a woman through the male lens, as we
have often seen. Reading the work of Laura Mulvey
can be helpful as can watching films that have been
written and/or directed by women in order to notice
differences in creative choices. Seeking feedback from
a trusted female friend, preferably also a writer, can
be of great benefit as well. Women bring something
special to the screen. Their stories are important.
Storytellers, both male and female, should be engaged
in telling them.

STRIPPING DOWN:
4 THINGS YOUR PROTAGONIST MAY HAVE TO
SHED TO SUCCEED

Guiding a character through a journey is a process of negotiating their inner desires and outer goals. While many films are constructed around the idea of a character that will gain one key thing over the course of the story, we sometimes forget that well-rounded characters will also lose some things along the way. Here are four things you may want to strip away from your protagonist as they make their way toward their goal.

Their Parents Or Home

Throughout the history of storytelling, characters have chosen to leave home in order to begin the journey they are called to. Joseph Campbell speaks at length about this in his work. Some have suggested that this is important for a character to do because all people relate to this decision. (Almost) every adult has made the choice to leave home at some point in order to begin his or her own life. Both Ben Gates (*National Treasure*) and Indiana Jones (*Indiana Jones and the Last Crusade*) leave behind disappointed fathers before taking off on their adventures. Luke Skywalker leaves his home planet to go and fight the Empire in *Star Wars: A New Hope.* Huck Finn runs away from home to raft down the Mississippi River. Mikey and his friends in *The Goonies* must ironically leave their parents and homes in order to ultimately save them. Even young Buddha leaves his father's palace to embark on his spiritual quest in the forest. Strong character development often begins with moving your protagonist out of their comfort zone and into more dangerous territory.

Their Crutches

Crutches can come in many forms. Friends, magic, shortcuts, masks, and comfort blankets can all be forms of crutches. Ultimately, a crutch is anything your protagonist uses to avoid having to face the thing what will bring the most change and development to their life. As wonderful as his powers are, Bruce Nolan cannot use them to save his marriage in *Bruce Almighty*. He must give up the magic he has been given in order to succeed at that. In *Pitch Perfect 2*, Beca and the Barton Bellas must give up their reliance on musical mashups and take a chance on original music in order to complete their journey. Anastasia Steele must give up her "comfort blanket" to go on her adventure with Mr. Grey in *50 Shades of Grey*.

Their Past

Sometimes, it's a "ghost" that still haunts them. Sometimes, it's the thing that has worked for them before. Sometimes, it's the memories they just can't stop thinking about. Like a snake in the spring, strong characters often must shed their old skin – the baggage they have traveled with for better or worse. Cheryl Strayed must shed the skin of her old life and the pain of her mother's death in *Wild*. Mac Radner and his wife must shed the polite tactics that have worked so well for them in the past in order to defeat the rowdy frat house next door in *Neighbors*. Prince Hakeem must hide the luxurious life he grew up with to find true love in *Coming to America*. In *The Judge*, Hank Palmer's slick courtroom presence must be put aside to achieve his inner goals. Even Joe Dirt must eventually give up the past he works the entire film to validate, in the story that bears his name.

What They Want, In Order To Get What They Need

Often, the thing the protagonist must shed is their reputation or what others think of them in order to truly be themselves. We see this in the journeys of Marty McFly (*Back to the Future*), Cady Heron (*Mean Girls*), and more recently in Ben Stiller's character, Josh, in *While We're Young*. In *The Imitation Game*, what Alan Turning wants is to be left alone to do his work privately. He must give this up in order to get what he truly needs – the acceptance that only comes through relationship. Sometimes, our protagonist must give up a physical object. Indiana Jones gives up the Holy Grail he searches for the entire film (*Indiana Jones and the Last Crusade*); in order to gain something he needs more desperately – the respect and acceptance of his father. In the end, asking our protagonist to give something up must always be for the greater good of granting them something even more valuable than what they had before. Sacrifice is always rewarded in powerful storytelling.

STORY POKER:
4 WAYS A CHARACTER CAN BLUFF

Are you a good liar? Do you avoid card games? Afraid your face will betray your hand? Just as we occasionally try to conceal the truth about ourselves, our characters often must do the same. Sometimes, our secrets are terrible, or at the very least embarrassing. Other times, we hide an ability we have, so that others might not ask us to use it. More than one IT professional has played dumb when a friend's computer went on the fritz. Perhaps you've kept your feelings of love or hate for someone a secret. Or maybe, you hide who you really are. As much as we might try to keep things to ourselves in real life, someone will always call our character's bluff in the world of story. Articulating how and why that plays out is one of our most important roles as writers. Here are four cards you might consider having your character keep close to the vest.

The Jack Of Spades:
The Dark Secret

Most people have at least one memory or event from their past they wish they could eliminate. Part of being human means showing our worst potential from time to time. Some of us spend our entire lives trying to make up for a mistake that still plagues us. Others choose to keep that mistake from ever seeing the light of day. Laney Brooks keeps secrets about her addiction to drugs and sex hidden from her husband and children in *I Smile Back*. Rudolph Abel goes to great lengths to keep what he has learned as a Russian spy in the United States under wraps in *Bridge of Spies*.

And *Spotlight*'s entire plot revolves around keeping a dark secret hidden. While these examples speak to dramatic scenarios, secrets can also make a wonderful basis for comedy. In *Knocked Up*, Allison tries to hide her pregnancy from her employers and friends. Steve Carrell keeps his virginity a secret from his co-workers in *The 40 Year Old Virgin*. Phil, Stu and Alan try to keep their buddy Doug's disappearance a secret from his fiancé in *The Hangover*. Bluffing keeps every one of these characters in the game, but not for long. Great dramatic conflict arises when the characters must finally show their cards.

The Ace:
The Rare Ability

Some of our most classic heroes in cinema have been reluctant heroes. We love to see someone with the ability to change a situation avoid doing so, at least for a short time. Of course, eventually we want to see our hero dive into the conflict. But we all understand wishing to avoid such commitments when possible. Often times in stories, as in real life, the person with the greatest ability to solve a problem is the last to agree to do so. Maximus is reluctant to take on leadership in Rome and eventually battle against the forces of Commodus in *Gladiator*. All he ever wanted was to return to a peaceful life with his wife and child. The story gets interesting, when Maximus is kept from his desires and forced to use his rare abilities. In *Dodgeball*, Kate Veatch's skills appear to only be as an accountant for the fledgling team she works for. However, she quickly reveals an amazing athletic ability that is key to helping the team win their tournament at the end of the story. Nearly all of the central characters in *Mad Max: Fury Road* are reluctant heroes that bluff each other until they must eventually combine their abilities to get what they want.

The Queen Of Hearts:
The True Desire

The tendency to hide our true feelings for someone we have deep interest in or hold with great contempt is common. With those we desire, we fear our feelings won't be reciprocated, so we bluff about the hearts we hold in our hand. With those we despise, we fear that the revelation of our feelings will cause conflict we don't wish to engage. Banky and Holden reveal secret desires at the end of *Chasing Amy* that puts their relationship in dire straights. In *Brokeback Mountain*, Ennis and Jack act on their hidden desires and then spend the rest of the story trying to deal with the fall-out. Caleb must work through the truth when he begins to desire an A.I. in *Ex Machina*. Nathan suspects this will be the case and uses Caleb's feelings in his own grand experiment. Ava, the A.I. has her own wishes that she keeps secret as well. In each of these stories, the true desires of the characters involved drive the action of the plot and are only revealed when the characters have the most to lose.

The Joker:
The Truth About Who They Really Are

We all wear many masks. We can easily slip one on and another off depending on our environment and those we come face to face with. Characters who bluff about who they really are, either inadvertently or explicitly, must eventually be unmasked. Wade Wilson cannot bear to unmask himself and reveal the truth to the love of his life, Vanessa, in *Deadpool*. He fears that what lies under his mask will be of greater significance than the love the two of them shared. In *How to Be Single*, Robin eventually reveals the truth about who she really is to great comedic and dramatic effect. Will wrestles with revealing the genius that resides inside him for a number of reasons in *Good Will Hunting*. *Unbreakable*, *The Wizard of Oz*, *Dogma*, *The Danish Girl*, and *Belle* all feature plots where key characters keep their true identity a secret.

Whatever secrets your character may keep throughout the course of the story only matter in the circumstances that they are revealed. The pay off of a revealed bluff only resonates with the audience if it is well-earned. The motivation behind the bluff as well as the consequences must be established early on in the story. If not, as writers we will find ourselves bluffing the audience about the cards we plan to play as the action unfolds.

STORYTELLING IN THE MENAGERIE:
4 WAYS ANIMALS CAN ASSIST IN SCRIPTWRITING

The relationship between animals and storytelling goes back to the very beginning. The narratives of early humans were often about the animals they hunted, the animals they feared, and the animals they worshipped. It's not surprising that the initial days of storytelling through film are filled with connections to animals as well. Perhaps the most significant of these connections is *The Horse in Motion* by Eadweard Muybridge. The result of a bet made by Leland Stanford, former governor of California, Muybridge photographed a horse galloping at high rates of speed and proved that there were moments when all four horse's feet were off the ground.

In Ang Lee's *Life of Pi*, Pi asks a novelist which of his stories the man prefers. "The one with the tiger. It's a better story," the man says. "So it is with God," Pi replies with a smile. There's something magical about the inclusion of animals in our stories. They can act as transcendent metaphors. They can create symbolism in otherwise straightforward stories. Their presence and interaction with us can teach us much about what it means to be human. Here are four uses of animals in the narrative that can add additional layers to your story.

Animals As Symbols

The use of animals in *The Life of Pi* could likely fill it's own book. However, one of the most significant is the tiger on the boat with Pi. The tiger can be seen as representative of the wild nature of the mystery of faith and religion that is juxtaposed against science in the story. The film continues to use animals to invoke this theme. We are challenged to consider that while science explains *how* the universe works, it fails to explain *why*. In *Inside Llewyn Davis*, the cat that Llewyn chases throughout the film symbolizes the success that seems to continually elude him. In *The Sopranos*, the migrating geese by Tony's pool symbolize his feelings about losses in his family. Every character in *The Royal Tenenbaums* has an animal associated with them. The philandering Royal Tenenbaum is symbolized by the havelina hung on his wall. When Royal is kicked out of the house, the havelina head comes down. It is restored to the wall when he returns home near the end of the film. Buckley, Mordecai, and Sparkplug are all symbols in the film for the deepest inner workings of the characters they accompany. In *The Wizard of Oz*, animal symbols are given an ironic twist when the Lion, traditionally a symbol of courage and strength in storytelling, proves to be a coward.

Animals As Us

When stories are centered around personified animals, it often allows us to see things about ourselves that we might not otherwise consider. Taking a story out of our literal world and into a world where animals speak and interact as we do can give us just enough separation from ourselves that our eyes can be truly opened. *The Muppets* make us laugh, but we can deeply relate to Kermit's longing for Miss Piggy. The loss of *Bambi*'s mother has brought more than one moviegoer to tears. This is not necessarily because we love animals so dearly, but more likely because we remember our own losses. *Babe, A Bug's Life, The Lion King, Rango, Alvin and the Chipmunks*, and *The Fantastic Mr. Fox* all allow us to look at ourselves through a different lens and see the animals featured in the stories as ourselves.

Animals As The Enemy

While animals have often been symbols of heroism that we project onto ourselves – see *Batman, Spiderman, Wolverine* and many others for examples – animals are sometimes also seen as our sworn enemies. *Jaws* still keeps many beach goers from setting foot in the water. Snakes have a rich ancient tradition of representing evil, but in *Anaconda,* the fear serpents can strike in us is imposingly amplified. *Arachnophobia* is a war between humans and spiders. *Congo* and *Planet of the Apes* pit us against primates. And *Deep Blue Sea, Lake Placid,* and the upcoming *In the Heart of the Sea* highlight the enemies we could encounter in the depths of the waters. Perhaps the most memorable of all stories about man versus beasts is *King Kong.* In every version of the film, a common trope of using animals as enemies is demonstrated – the revelation that they are actually just misunderstood creatures. This, of course, is an important universal question at the heart of humanity. Are those things we fear truly deserving of our distress or are they simply things we have failed to rightly understand?

Animals As Friends

There is a rich tradition of stories that speak of animals being loyal companions. Seeing this theme reinforced reminds us of the animals who have meant so much to us in our own lives. These stories often feature a character who is having trouble fitting in

– a symbolic "fish out of water." An animal shows up, befriends our struggling hero and gives them the confidence they need to face the challenges ahead of them. *Free Willy, Air Bud, The Black Stallion, Black Beauty,* and *Beethoven* all utilize animals as meaningful friends to humans. *Ace Ventura: Pet Detective* accomplishes the same in a much more humorous fashion. Even the great Tom Hanks has chosen to tell a story of this sort – *Turner and Hooch.* Very little set up has to be given in a story before we understand the relationship regarding a person and how much an animal means to them.

From *Drive* and *Silence of the Lambs*, to *Big Fish* and *Old Yeller,* animals have meaning in stories because animals have meaning to *us.* Using them in our storytelling can help us communicate to an audience less clumsily and more figuratively. As animals have been useful to us in the world since the dawn of time, they continue to be in the worlds we construct in our minds.

THE REVERSE RUBE GOLDBERG:
4 WAYS TO BRING COMPLEX MATERIAL
TO AN AUDIENCE

Most people's familiarity with Rube Goldberg machines comes from Bugs Bunny cartoons. These comical appliances take a simple task and create an incredibly complex process around it. Several films have memorable opening scenes where Rube Goldbergs are seen. *Back to the Future* and *Pee Wee's Big Adventure* open with incredibly convoluted home made technologies that make breakfast and feed pets. Many times, as writers, we are attempting to do just the opposite. We need to take a massively complex issue or story, and simplify it to a point where our audience can engage and enjoy it. But how do we go about doing that? Here are four methods for bringing complex material to your audience.

Take A Small Aspect Of The Larger Story And Explain It

This technique has been used a great deal as of late. Rather than trying to give us a biopic of Abraham Lincoln's life, *Lincoln* focuses on two pivotal weeks of the President's career. Lincoln's journey and the complexities surrounding slavery and the Civil War would be far too much for any feature film to structure around. *Suffragette* takes the same approach with the women's suffrage movement. Rather than trying to detail the intricacies of the struggle, they instead focus on one woman's story in the midst of the conflict. In *Do The Right Thing*, race relations in New York City are explored through the journey of a pizza deliveryman. The entire story takes place on a single day (compressed time) on a single block (compressed space) in New York. Race relations in any major city are surely complex. Bringing these complications down to a manageable size helps the audience to digest how the lessons of these smaller stories apply at higher levels as well.

Focus On One Character's Perspective

The work of Robert Altman and Paul Thomas Anderson has made every screenwriter want to try their hand at the ensemble story at least once. Pulling these stories off successfully is an achievement that few writers can master. Unless you have years of storytelling experience under your belt, focusing on one or two characters and their perspectives in complex situations is more advisable.

The rise, successes and failures in the tech industry are a complex narrative, to be sure. *Silicon Valley* features a wide array of comical characters that make the tale more interesting. However, the intricate story is clearly from the perspective of Richard Hendricks. *Spotlight* unravels the Boston Clergy sex abuse scandal in a mesmerizing way. The case is handled by a team of reporters, all who bring layers to the story, in unique ways. However, *Spotlight* is from the perspective of the head of the team, Robby Robinson. There is a delicate balance that must be maintained when telling stories about complex situations. It often requires the use of many characters. The trick is to keep the perspective from one character clear and allow the other characters to challenge, change, or support that perspective.

Use Metaphor

Writers have taken complex emotions, scenarios, and people and portrayed them with metaphor for centuries. Sometimes the easiest way to understand something or someone is by understanding a similar idea. Angela Hayes, the cheerleader that Lester Burnham fixates on in *American Beauty*, is a metaphor for the youth and vitality that Lester feels he is losing. The Winklevoss twins in *The Social Network* are metaphors for the corporate structure that tried to stomp out the entrepreneurial success of social media. Baseball is used as a metaphor for the universal desires we all have about safety, leisure, and happiness in *Traffic*. Sometimes the easiest way to make a complex idea simple is to state it indirectly. Metaphor gives us the power to do just that.

Break The 4Th Wall And Directly Explain It

Let us return for a moment to the proverbial 4th wall. This technique should be used with caution. It can serve as the calling card of a lazy writer or at least a writer who lacks the skills to use another technique for making a complex idea simple. However, when used as an organic or creative aspect of the narrative, it can be quite engaging. Explaining the housing crisis of 2007 is a tough goal for any story. In *The Big Short*, Jared Vennett occasionally breaks the 4th wall and has a celebrity, such as Margot Robbie, explain a complexity to the audience directly. The approach feels fresh thanks to the execution. Philippe Petit breaks the 4th wall and explains his inner feelings and motivations to the audience throughout the story in *The Walk*. This approach actually helps us understand why someone would undertake such a deadly activity. In *The Diary of a Teenage Girl*, Minnie breaks the 4th wall in order to make her case to those in the audience who would question the wisdom of a teenage girl having an affair with an older man. It's important to remember that this approach will not work for every story. It is a technique that should only be used when the narrative is actually better served by employing its power.

4 WAYS TO IMPROVE YOUR INCITING INCIDENT

Every story needs one, but it can be one of the most misunderstood elements in scriptwriting. It's called by many names – catalyst, initiating beat, and inciting incident are just a few. How well you can engage the viewer in that exact moment often determines whether a reader will keep turning pages in your script or move on to something more interesting. Here are four ways to improve the inciting incident in your story.

Stick It In The Right Spot

One of the most common errors I see in scripts from new writers is the misplaced inciting incident. I've read ten-page, short film scripts where the inciting incident occurred at the bottom of the sixth page. I've read just as many features where the moment occurs in an equally bad spot. A common rule of thumb from story gurus of the past has been to have the inciting incident occur around page ten in a feature, or when the story has been roughly ten percent told, regardless of the script's length. This is not a bad place to start. Many scripts now open with an inciting incident and build set up after it occurs. This model works well, too. The more dangerous method is waiting too late for an inciting incident. Waiting until the 15% or 20% mark in the story can bore or confuse an audience. This is all assuming we are telling a linear story, of course. In *Selma*, President Johnson tells Martin Luther King, Jr. that the voting act will have to wait. This is the inciting incident that drives King to go to Selma. Writer, Paul Webb has this occur eleven minutes into the film – right on time.

Make It A Day Like No Other

I sometimes refer to the inciting incident as "the phone call that changes your life." The inciting incident often works best when it occurs on the most significant day of your protagonist's life. It might be the day someone they love dies. It might be the day they lost their job or their husband left them. It might be the day they found a magic box that could make their dreams come true. One helpful exercise is to look at an inciting incident from your own life. How was life different when you went to bed that night as opposed to when you got up? Our protagonist can decide whether they will go on the journey later. The inciting incident should create the circumstances that force the decision they will later make. In *The Theory of Everything,* it's not Stephen Hawking's medical diagnosis that serves as the inciting incident but instead his meeting Jane. Writer, Anthony McCarten is arguing that it's this moment that changed Hawking's life more than any other. The script goes on to make a very compelling argument for that point.

Make It Personal

The inciting incident should eventually lead the protagonist to make a decision between two very appealing choices or two very awful choices. For this reason, the moment must be personal. The character must have a lot to gain or a lot to lose based on the situation created by the inciting incident. The more extreme the situation, the higher the dramatic conflict in the story will be. Has your protagonist just lost what they loved most? Do they now posses the means to have all they ever wanted? Has the man of their dreams just been hired by the company they work for? Whatever the inciting incident, nothing should be the same for your protagonist after it occurs. Cheryl Strayed's character in *Wild* is never the same after her mother dies. Though the film used a somewhat non-linear storytelling style, writer, Nick Hornby makes it quite clear that this event is Strayed's inciting incident for all she goes on the accomplish. For her, nothing was more personal than processing that tragedy.

Let It Breathe

After the inciting incident occurs, the protagonist needs a moment to exhale. Don't immediately rush into another story beat. Give the heroine time to react – time to catch their breath. One effective method is to provide a sounding board for them. Having a conversation occur with a mentor or close friend can allow the character to explore the pros and cons of going on the journey that the inciting incident has made available. But don't linger here. Waiting too long to have the protagonist make their decision to engage the journey can bore the audience. We lose our empathy for the predicament the character is in if they appear to be wallowing in indecision. In *The Imitation Game*, writer Graham Moore allows Alan Turing's character to both positively react to the inciting incident (which occurs on page ten of the script, by the way) of being called in to work on a secret project and negatively react to the people he will be working with. The tension between these two realities is what makes Turing's decision to work on the project a difficult one. As Moore demonstrates, a great inciting incident can accomplish multiple purposes and develop the character from the beginning of the story.

4 WAYS TO OPEN YOUR STORY WITH A BANG

More than any other scene, the opening sequence of your story must be captivating. It must intrigue us in some way. But what about the very first image the audience sees? Are there ways to master visual storytelling that entrances the viewer from the very first second light hits the screen? Here are four ways to do it.

Begin With An Image that Shocks or Provokes the Audience

Why waste a single second trying to arrest your audience's attention or imagination? Opening with an image that moves the viewer to the edge of their seat can be one way to get them onboard immediately with your story. It will be important to keep your audience's attention through pacing and strategic inhales and exhales in the plot. But don't be afraid to hit the audience hard from the opening frame. In *True Story*, it's not James Franco or Jonah Hill that we see first. Instead, we are jolted by the image of fluffy teddy bear falling on top of a dead child, who has been stuffed inside a suitcase. While not for the faint of heart, it's an image that any viewer won't soon forget. We know a horrible crime has been committed. We immediately feel that whoever has committed this crime deserves the most harsh punishment imaginable. We know enough backstory to go on the journey before us. *Fight Club*'s opening shot is less morbid but no less shocking. Edward Norton's character sits staring right into the camera, eyes wide and sweat dripping down his brow -- with a gun in his mouth. We immediately begin to question who Norton is, who is holding the gun, and what led to such dire circumstances.

Begin With an Image that Creates a World Without a Single Word of Dialogue

Storytelling for the screen is by nature a visual medium. Finding ways to tell the story through images rather than words is an essential skill for anyone wanting to master the craft. While you'll have plenty of opportunity to work in clever dialogue and amazing one-liners, try opening your story with no words at all. In *Super 8*, the first image we see is a sign that indicates the number of days a factory has worked without injuries. A hand moves into frame placing a number 1 on the sign. We know that tragedy must have struck the day before. We know this will be a story about people coping with this in some way and perhaps trying to pick up the pieces. The tone of the world we are entering is clearly established. Similarly, in *Star Wars: A New Hope,* the first image we see is that of a small craft fleeing a much larger spaceship. The larger ship is blasting the smaller with firepower. We know this will be a story about underdogs. The world of this story is ruled by a much larger force that is in the business of wiping out any rebel insurgents, no matter how small. All this is accomplished without a single word of dialogue.

Begin With an Abstract Image that Communicates a Major Theme of the Story

Worried about being too on the nose with your opening image? Try beginning with a visual that's more abstract but will later have significance. In *Woman in Gold,* we see tight shots of Gustav Klimt's hands crafting his masterpiece painting Lady in Gold. Klimt's unusual technique of applying gold to his painting sparks our curiosity as to what exactly is being created and what the significance of this creation will be. All this is eventually paid off in the story. Even the crafting of the gold to the canvas serves as visual metaphor for the internal journey that Ryan Reynolds's character takes throughout the course of the film. Proving that this technique is not just effective on the big screen, we can recall how TV juggernaut *Breaking Bad* also used this same method. The first movement we see on screen in the saga of Walter White is a pair of khaki pants falling from the skies to the ground – a wonderful metaphor for the plunge this vanilla suburbanite is about to take over the next several years.

Begin Without an Image

It's a risky thing to let an audience sit in complete darkness for any length of time. It can be jarring and even one second, when the screen is black, plays three times longer in a theater full of people. It can, however, be an incredible attention-grabber. In *Inherent Vice*, the poetic voice of a woman guides us through the darkness into the world we will spend the remainder of the film reconciling. The same technique is used in *Kill Bill: Vol. 1*. Over black, we hear Bill's voice and another character's heavy breathing, asking us "Do you find me sadistic?" In both cases, there is a small relief in the viewer's mind when an image does finally appear on-screen. We know that the darkness is over and we will now journey into the story. Used sparingly, the lack of images can be a captivating technique in visual storytelling.

A TIME TO KILL:
5 CHARACTERS YOU CAN EXTERMINATE

There's been a tremendous amount of discussion about killing characters recently, as HBO revealed whether a key character on *Game of Thrones* was actually dead or alive. The discussion had merit, as HBO, and especially *Game of Thrones*, has a habit of killing off significant characters in their narratives. Obviously, any conversation about killing key characters is going to be clothed in spoilers – so reader beware. Death, of course, is a universal experience in life. Everyone will die. However, knowing if, who, and when to kill characters in your story can be a high stakes game. Here are five character archetypes you might consider killing in your script.

Kill the Mentor

One of the chief goals when creating a character in a story is to build empathy for him or her. Taking away someone they love is a powerful way of accomplishing this. Every person either has lost or will lose someone they love. We all know how it feels. It's hard to dislike a character who goes through this experience. Of course, before we take away a mentor, we have to establish how much they mean to our protagonist. We have to take time in the story to demonstrate relationship. We often want to show our protagonist butting up against the advice or training of the mentor, before they see the wisdom that was taught. These things take time in a story. Killing a mentor is usually not a good idea to consider unless you are at least half way through your story. You also don't want to wait too late to kill the mentor. You must give your character time to respond to the mentor's death and then to use the wisdom they offered. Mick, *Rocky*'s mentor, doesn't die until the third installment of the series. Obi Wan Kenobi and Yoda both die, but only after they have invested in Luke Skywalker in the *Star Wars* saga. Not all mentors fit the wise old sage trope. Royal Tenenbaum is practically the opposite of Obi Wan Kenobi, but still manages to teach his family lessons before his death at the end of the story.

Kill the Protagonist

When we talk about killing a character in our stories, our minds immediately gravitate to the possibility of killing the protagonist. While this can be an effective strategy in storytelling, it's not one without risks. Killing the main character takes perfect narrative timing. In the minds of many audience members, once the person they consider to be the main character dies, the story is over. For this reason, many storytellers wait till the end of the film to kill off their protagonist. Ben in *Seven Pounds*, Gatsby in *The Great Gatsby*, and William Wallace in *Braveheart* all die, but not until the end of the story. More recently, a few storytellers have experimented with killing main characters earlier in their narratives. Bill Pope in *Criminal* and Luke in *The Place Beyond the Pines* both die early on in their stories. *Malcom X, Saving Private Ryan, Into the Wild, American Beauty*, and *Gladiator* all kill off their protagonists in different ways.

Kill the Antagonist

Much more common than killing off the protagonist is the idea of killing off the antagonist. There's a catharsis the audience feels when the antagonist gets what is coming to them. Unsurprisingly, many storytellers use this built-in emotion to conclude their stories. Rarely, if ever do we see the antagonist die before the end of the story. When John Fitzgerald is left to die in *The Revenant*, Hugh Glass's journey feels complete. When Javert dies at the end of *Les Misrables*, Jean Valjean is finally free of the weight he has carried throughout the story. The look on Jack Torrance's dead face at the end of *The Shining* is somehow just as chilling as the moment he breaks through the door with an axe. Seeing Hans Gruber descend into oblivion at the conclusion of *Die Hard* makes us all feel like John McClane.

Kill the Lovers

There's perhaps no love story more well-known than *Romeo and Juliet.* The timeless tale ends with both lovers dead. While it's not necessary for *both* lovers to die in order to build empathy with the audience, taking away something one character values greatly is impactful, and has an even greater effect than taking away a character such as the mentor. Jack Dawson's icy death in *Titanic* breaks our hearts because we know what he meant to Rose. Satine's death in *Moulin Rouge* has a similar impression on Christian. *Atonement, A Walk to Remember*, and *Leaving Las Vegas* all portray the deaths of either one or both of the lovers involved. Even *Forrest Gump* brings a tear to our eye when he gives us the details about the death of his beloved Jenny.

Kill Everyone

From Greek tragedies through Shakespeare, there's
a long tradition of killing off nearly all the characters
in a story. This plot device only works in certain
types of stories and can risk alienating the audience.
However, many narratives accomplish great things
and still manage to end the lives of most if not all the
characters in the story. In *Green Room*, only Pat and
Amber are left standing after an army of friends and
enemies meet their demise. Both *Thelma and Louise*
cruise into the great beyond together at the conclusion
of their story. Nearly every character in *The Departed*
dies before the film is over. Historical films often lean
on the true stories of massive deaths. *Butch Cassidy
and the Sundance Kid, Bonnie and Clyde, Young
Guns II*, and *Platoon* are but a few examples where
nearly all main characters meet their fate. Of course,
no discussion about killing off characters would
be complete without honoring the work of Quinten
Tarantino. *Reservoir Dogs, Inglorious Basterds, The
Hateful Eight*, and most of QT's other films all kill off a
great number of the cast before the final credits roll.

FACES OF DEATH:
5 DEATHS A HERO MAY EXPERIENCE

No one gets out of here alive. While it sounds like a line from the latest Tarantino film, it's a universal truth that every person must come to terms with. We will all die. There are no exceptions. Dealing with death is one of the most difficult tasks our humanity requires of us. It's no surprise that we use art to deal with this difficulty. While physical death is a bridge every person will cross, there are other deaths that only a select few will experience. Even if you aren't writing *The Hateful Eight*, here are five different deaths your hero may have to face.

Death of Desires

One of the most classic methods in scriptwriting is forcing a character to give up what she wants for what she needs. It's important to establish a character's wants early in the story. In fact, it's essential if we are to care about the character we are watching. Throughout the course of the second act, we should see that character fight for what they want. We should see others try to take it from them. We should see them come close to getting what they want only to have it slip between their fingers. In the third act, we may see them actually get what they want. But we may not. We may see them let their desire for what they want die in order to receive something much greater – what they need. The death of desire is rarely about giving up. Instead, it is about coming to a greater realization about what their desires. Perhaps the desire was selfish. Perhaps the desire was petty. Perhaps it just wasn't worth the cost. In *The 40 Year*

Old Virgin, Steve Carrel's character lets his desire
to lose his virginity die in order to truly get to know
the woman he is dating. In the end, his desire is
resurrected and he gets both what he wants and what
he needs. The same arc occurs in *Knocked Up* with
Seth Rogen's character.

Death of Pride

Many times, the death that a character must face will
occur inside them. Aside from being one of the seven
deadly sins, pride can be an Achilles heel for even the
most likable character. We are forgiving of pride, since
we all deal with it, as long as a character eventually
lets it die in the third act of the story. There is
something very cathartic about seeing a character let
their pride die. It gives us permission and assurance
about letting our own pride perish. Laying down one's
pride is always a process. The same is true for our
characters. We can't see them give this up too easily.
Characters must fight for their pride. They should only
give it up when all other options have been explored.
It should hurt and perhaps nearly kill them in the
process. Michael B. Jordan fights with his own pride
throughout *Creed*. It's only after he manages to give
it up that he gets the things he truly needs. Lindsay
Lohan faces the same battle inside a high school,
rather than a boxing ring, in *Mean Girls*. Overcoming
her pride not only solves the key battle raging within
her, but also brings peace to all those around her.

Death of Dreams

While in films such as *Les Miserables*, we see Anne
Hathaway's character suffer the final death of her

dreams, other stories allow a character's dreams to
die and later be resurrected. Structurally, if a dream
is to be resurrected, it should die in the first act so
it can rise again in the third. Occasionally, we will
see a dream die at the end of the second act to rise
again in the third. This does have less punch and
works better for secondary characters. It can also
work in a comedy if the character's dream is not the
central external goal in the story. In *Joy*, Jennifer
Lawrence sees her dreams crushed at a young
age. They are later resurrected and become her
salvation. Jason Schwartzman's dreams die when he
is kicked out of his beloved *Rushmore*. However, we
see them resuscitated in a new environment by the
story's conclusion. *Field of Dreams*, *The Shawshank
Redemption*, and *Slumdog Millionaire* all base their
central conflicts around the death of dreams.

Death of Loved Ones

While many of us can come to terms with our own
demise, it's the death of those we love that we struggle
with most intensely. We can live cautiously, eat
healthy, and avoid all danger for ourselves. But we
have no control over the fate of those we care most
about. Watching a character wrestle with the loss of
a loved one or even the potential loss of a loved one
can bring even the strongest hero to their knees.
Tom Cruise's character in *Magnolia* is one of the
most arrogant and disgusting people we could ever
encounter until he comes face to face with his dying
father in a moment that completely humanizes him.
In *The Revenant*, Leonardo DiCaprio's loss of his son
breaks him. He spends the entire story surviving
only to avenge this death. *Ordinary People, Good Will*

Hunting, and *Ray* all feature characters trying to come to terms with the death of loved ones.

Death Of Body

As discussed, it's a dangerous proposition to have a main character die in a story. It can be highly effective or it can cause you to lose your audience. If a main character does die, it becomes important to have other central characters survive, at least for a short time, in order to deal with the death of the main character. In *The Danish Girl*, Eddie Redmayne risks his very life to become who his character knows she is inside. In the end, the character dies a triumphant death, having sacrificed everything for her truth. Alicia Vikander provides us the perspective of life after the death of our hero. *The Iron Giant* sacrifices his metal body in order to save the people he has come to care about. Their reaction to his sacrifice tells us a great deal about the impact of his life. *Me and Earl and the Dying Girl* uses a similar method of storytelling.

Death is a given in life. It's one of the most universal subjects we can explore in our storytelling. If we can be truthful about its effects, its meaning, and those it leaves behind, we will touch the audience in a way that few subjects can.

WHAT CAN YOU DO FOR ME?
5 QUALITIES TO MAKE YOUR MAIN
CHARACTER COMPELLING

Characters are compelling for the same reasons
humans are. We are, after all, characters. Just less
crafted than the ones we see on screen. When we have
qualities, talents, and abilities that distinguish who
we are from those around us, people tend to find us
interesting. Giving your characters unique abilities
or superpowers is certainly one way to capture the
attention of the audience. However, most times this
only works if you are writing in a specific genre or
creating a certain type of story. We often overlook the
fact that there are qualities that are unique but not
TOO unique in people we encounter everyday. Here are
five qualities that can give your character an upgrade
in the personality department.

THE CRACKERJACK
The Ability to Crack Things

Most of us are fascinated by someone who can pick
a lock or solve a difficult puzzle. The ability to do so
usually indicates years of experience, training, or
preparation. We enjoy seeing those years pay off as it
gives us hope that our own experiences have prepared
us for the difficulties we will have to maneuver through
in life. In *The Goonies*, Mikey and his crew crack riddle
after riddle to eventually uncover the treasures of One
Eyed Willy. Sherlock Holmes made a career, not to
mention many wonderful adventures, out of solving
difficult puzzles. Less obvious, however, is Joel Barish
in *Eternal Sunshine of the Spotless Mind*, who goes
to great lengths to solve his own mystery. Quentin in

Paper Towns does the same, interpreting clue after clue to track down his beloved Margo.

THE FIXER
The Ability to Fix or Repair Things

Similar to the ability to crack things, the ability to fix things reassures us that training and preparation pay off in the end. All of us know and likely admire someone who is good with his or her hands. It could be an aunt who you call when your car breaks down or a brother that understands the ways of the latest Windows operating system. Often equally valuable are those who know how to fix situations. There are those who can offer just the right words to us when our hearts are broken and pillars of wisdom who can navigate us through the most wicked of life's labyrinths. Winston Wolfe shows up in *Pulp Fiction* telling Vincent and Jules that he's there to help and if they listen to him, they might all get out of the situation alive. In *Sling Blade*, Karl Childers shares his ability to repair lawnmowers as well as broken homes. Sometimes, what needs repair is inside us, however. Ray Kinsella repairs a number of broken relationships, including his own, in *Field of Dreams*. Grace dedicates her life to repairing the broken lives of kids in a group home in *Short Term 12*.

THE GREASE MAN
The Ability to Get Out of Tight Fixes

Some people have the ability to seemingly escape any situation. They are smooth talkers who can maneuver through life's most difficult obstacle courses with grace and ease. Whether relying on their brain, their brawn, or both, these characters always have a solution when things seem impossible. Ethan Hunt personifies this in the *Mission Impossible* films. Danny Ocean does the same in the *Ocean's Eleven* franchise. James Bond is perhaps the most well known of the grease men. In films such as *From Russia With Love,* Bond demonstrates there is likely no fix he can't find his way out of. Maya and Dan make their way through the direst of circumstances to eventually capture Osama Bin Laden in *Zero Dark Thirty.* Demonstrating that the grease man doesn't solely exist in the action genre, Mark Zuckerberg performs verbal gymnastics to get out of tight fix after tight fix in *The Social Network.*

MR. NEVER IN DOUBT
Having Extreme Confidence

Most of us try to make sure our confidence level floats somewhere around where our actual ability level is. When characters let this balance slide to one extreme or another, the results are dramatic, and often comedic. In *Vacation,* Clark Griswold (and now his son Rusty, in the newest version of the series) is often wrong but never in doubt. He makes error after error. But what truly makes these predicaments funny is the confidence he barrels into every situation with. Michael Scott, of the TV classic *The Office,* is another fine example of a character whose confidence creates chaos all around him. However, Scott never seems too bothered by his own track record of calamities. *Airplane!* is a film full of humorous characters with extreme confidence issues. As is Leslie Nielsen's *Naked Gun* series. In *Ferris Bueller's Day Off,* Ferris proves that extreme confidence isn't only for the buffoon. *Gladiator* and *Philomena* both offer dramatic lead characters with extreme confidence, proving this quality can be a basis for more than humor.

THE DOUBTING THOMAS
Having Extreme Lack of Confidence

Much the opposite of Mr. Never In Doubt, The Doubting Thomas creates drama with his extreme lack of confidence. Andy in *The 40 Year Old Virgin* makes a lack of confidence compelling, and of course humorous. Peter Bretter does the same in *Forgetting Sarah Marshall*. More subtly, lead characters in *Adventureland*, *Mr. Smith Goes to Washington*, and *Never Been Kissed* give us compelling stories of those who overcome their extreme lack of confidence. In *Superbad*, Seth and Evan openly discuss their confidence issues and how they plan to overcome them, hoping to become "some girl's mistake." Often times, we become privy to what caused a knock out blow to the character's confidence. In *The Wedding Singer*, the first act of the film is dedicated to the backstory behind why Robby suffers with confidence issues. All of us experience doubt in ourselves, it's only when this doubt affects a character's life in a way that causes chaos and conflict that we can use it to develop who that character is and how they can change.

BUILDING FRANKENSTEIN:
5 PIECES OF MATERIAL WITH WHICH TO
CONSTRUCT YOUR CHARACTER

Here are five pieces of material to use when constructing your Frankenstein.

Physical Material

Perhaps the most obvious material to use when constructing a character is the physical elements that give them their appearance. This material might not be necessary for every character, but it is often an opportunity to create interest in the mind of the audience or make the character unique. Elijah Price is far more interesting in *Unbreakable* because he is in a wheel chair. His physical appearance connects to his backstory, which makes the creative choice feel organic, and not at all arbitrary. Her enemies never see Susan Cooper coming in *Spy*. This is thanks to her physical appearance, which also provides lots of comedic opportunity, as Cooper's exterior is not what we expect for an international spy. It's easy to randomly assign physical attributes to a character in order to make them more interesting. However, physical material is most successful when it is tied to another one of the materials – psychological, backstory, desire, or detail.

Psychological Material

This material can be tricky. It's a slippery slope trying to reveal what a character is thinking or who they are on the inside. James Donovan must maintain a certain psychological demeanor when dealing with Rudolf Abel in *Bridge of Spies*. We only begin to understand what he really thinks of Abel and how his inner psychology is functioning as he interacts with his wife and colleagues. Revealing psychology through encounters and relationships with others can be a clever way to tell us about a character. However, you must avoid the snare of allowing your character to easily state what's going on inside them through dialogue. *Show* us what your character is thinking. Avoid just *telling* us. Often the psychological material we use to build a character comes out of a flaw or fear. Mark Baum's motivations are born of his imperfections in *The Big Short*. This is slowly revealed through the character's actions over the course of the story as opposed to being told to the audience through a few lines of dialogue.

Backstory Material

What a character experienced before your story begins is the key to developing a "ghost" for the character. Having an issue or event haunt that character gives them motivation they are likely not to want to discuss. This presents a challenge for the writer but is more rewarding for the audience when they discover what has been plaguing the character throughout the narrative. P.L. Travers is reluctant to make changes to her beloved Mary Poppins in *Saving Mr. Banks*. It's not until much later we discover that her reasons involve things that happened long before the story being told began. Furiosa is "haunted" in a similar fashion in *Mad Max: Fury Road*. Many writers will write pages of backstory for a character that never make it in to the narrative they are crafting. The reason behind such an exercise is for the creator to truly get to know the creation. Characters are made multi-dimensional only when the writer knows the character and their history, both inside and out.

Desire Material

Knowing what a character wants is essential if an audience is to engage your story. Establishing what they *need* should be revealed over the course of their internal journey, but knowing what they *want* should be established early on. In *Trumbo*, Dalton Trumbo simply desires to keep working while expressing his beliefs. His desire reveals to us his character. It reveals who he is internally. It tells us much about his psychology and perhaps even his backstory. Carol Aird desires Therese Belivet in *Carol*. Her desire, however, doesn't just reveal to us a sexual preference. It reveals a longing for a life she cannot have in her current culture and situation. In this case, her desire reveals the conflict of the story. The more intensely a character wants something, the higher the audience's sense of engagement will be. The more they are willing to sacrifice, the greater our empathy will be.

Detailed Material

Crafting details about a character takes precision and nuance. Knowing what particulars reveal more of who the character is as opposed to simply communicating more information should be in the wheelhouse of an experienced storyteller. Ted Cole gives a wonderful monologue about the importance of a tennis shoe brand in *The Door in the Floor* in order to demonstrate the importance of detail when constructing a character. A key character in *The Revenant* carries a dented canteen. This detail becomes a crucial plot point later in the story. A flourish of blood, on a white helmet, from the fingers of a dead storm trooper, help us follow the story of the character who will later become Finn in *Star Wars: The Force Awakens*.

Combining the elements of physical traits, psychological material, backstory, desire and details, you can bring a character to life. But remember, human beings don't always act rationally. They aren't constructed like formulas. It's important to surprise the audience with irony, unexpected choices, and brokenness. We are more than the sum total of our parts. Your characters should be as well.

5 LESSONS FROM 2015'S OSCAR NOMS FOR BEST ORIGINAL SCREENPLAY

Oscar season is upon us. Studios are putting their best foot forward in attempts to woo us with the finest stories they have to offer. While it's tempting to begin guessing what films will be selected for next year's highest honors, it's worth taking a look back at the original scripts that rose to be nominated this year. There are lessons to be learned from the stories that were told. Here are five story principles we can take from the 2015 Oscar nominees for best Original Screenplay.

Experimentation Can Work: Boyhood

While there are tried and true forms that cause scripts to resonate with the human psyche, there will always be a place for experimentation that can expand the art form. Richard Linklater demonstrated with *Boyhood* that experimentation can pay off greatly under the direction of a master. While Linklater had the basis for the story in his head, the script was written over the same period that the film was made. His grand experiment of filmmaking captivated audiences. Watching a boy grow up before our eyes was a unique novelty, but it was only great art because the novelty was hung on a masterfully told story. Over the years, films ranging from *Pulp Fiction* to *(500) Days of Summer* to *Synecdoche, New York* have utilized experimental storytelling to great effect.

Internal Journeys Need External Frameworks: Foxcatcher

Max Frye and Dan Futterman chose to tell a very nuanced story with *Foxcatcher*. It was the type of script that actors salivate over. It was not over-written, and allowed the talent lots of room to interpret the characters. If you've read the script, it's no wonder that the likes of Steve Carrell, Channing Tatum, and Mark Ruffalo signed on. Each of the three main characters in the story are traveling through a complex inner journey. The journey happens to take place in the world of wrestling, but *Foxcatcher* is certainly not a movie about the sport. Many writers are attracted to stories of inner journeys but lack the skills to frame the narrative in a world that metaphorically expresses the path inside the characters. Inner chronicles have hooked audiences since the beginning of storytelling. However, it cannot be overstated how important it is to find an external framework that will keep the audience interested while the protagonist battles their inner demons. *American Beauty, Brokeback Mountain,* and *Rushmore* are all examples of stories that offer inner journeys through interesting external frameworks.

Tension Can Rise When Dialogue is Sparse: Nightcrawler

There are many moments in *Nightcrawler* when Louis Bloom's character is silent. We see him examining horrific events. The tension in these scenes rises greatly because writer, Dan Gilroy, chose to keep the protagonist silent. Bloom seems to choose his words very carefully in the story. When he does speak, our blood pressure rises. Beginning writers often make the mistake of having their characters speak too often. Finding a rhythm for the pace of dialogue comes with practice, but is a necessary discipline for effective storytellers. It can be a healthy exercise to examine your script and locate every time the protagonist speaks. Ask yourself if this line of dialogue moves the plot forward in any way? Does it reveal character? Does it serve a purpose in the scene? Just like in life, people in scripts often speak without really having anything to say. *Sling Blade*, *Taxi Driver*, and *Winter's Bone* all tells stories of protagonists that choose their conversations with others wisely and infrequently.

Settings Can Be Their Own Characters: The Grand Budapest Hotel

Let's face it, Wes Anderson can get away with many things the average storyteller cannot, because he does it with such style. One technique that Anderson does employ, that's available to us all, is his use of locales as characters in his stories. While filled with witty and eccentric characters, *The Grand Budapest Hotel* its self plays its own distinctive role in the film. A story's setting can be just as intriguing to audiences as the people inhabiting that world. This is a secret writers in the science fiction and action genres have known for decades. What makes Anderson's approach interesting is that he uses the hotel as a character in a comedy, a less likely genre for such a tactic. *Titanic*, *Straight Outta Compton*, and *Little Miss Sunshine* all use settings as characters.

Give Me the Same Thing Only Different: Birdman Or (The Unexpected Virtue Of Ignorance)

In many ways, Alejandro Inarritu's masterpiece is the last story we would associate with the "same things" we've seen before. It feels fresh and original. In many other ways, however, the story is one we have definitely heard before. It's a story about a super hero. It's a story about an actor who's facing growing older. It's a story about a man with a clear enemy. It's a story about an individual at odds with people he loves. It's not that *Birdman* is a story we've never experienced. What makes it unique is that it's a story we can relate to, told in a *way* we've never seen before. The Academy often favors stories that provide a new twist on an old tale. This was quite possibly why this story took home the gold statue in February. Remember, as writers, we don't need to reinvent the wheel. We just need to decorate the wheel in a way no one has seen before. *Precious*, *Juno*, and *Kiss Kiss Bang Bang* are all stories that provide a new twist on a classic narrative.

5 LESSONS IN STORYTELLING FROM BILL MURRAY

The entertainment industry is filled with legends about the process for casting Bill Murray in a film. It's no secret that the comedic genius is choosy about the stories he agrees to inhabit. So what can we learn about the cinematic choices he's made? Here are five lessons in storytelling we can learn from Bill Murray films.

Lovable Losers Always Win Us Over

Many of Murray's characters are down on their luck, socially awkward, or overly confident in their abilities, and in a word --losers. Murray knows that audiences identify strongly with characters that wear their flaws on their sleeve. In his most recent film, *Rock the Kasbah,* Murray encounters terrorists, arms dealers, and rogue prostitutes. While the setup creates an environment fit for James Bond, BM portrays Richie Lanz, an over the hill rock promoter who hasn't had a successful client in years. Lanz talks a big game, but is never able to actually deliver on his aspirations. It's only at the end of the story when Lanz admits that he's not all he claims to have been that he can rise to the ranks of a real hero and make the difference in people's lives he's always longed for.

Cranky Characters Carry Potential

Bill Murray is the master of the cranky character. He doesn't have to utter a word of dialogue to convince us of the chip on his shoulder. Murray has figured out the key to why cranky characters work so well in stories. The explanation lies in that audiences respond so strongly to seeing a cranky character find even the slightest bit of joy, which Murray's characters always seem to do by the end. When we see cranky characters find some delight, we believe that it might exist for us as well. In *Scrooged*, Murray portrays Frank Cross. Cross is a cranky boss who makes his employees work late into the night on Christmas eve. When Cross learns the true meaning of the holiday season at the end of the story, we find ourselves celebrating right along with him. Murray pulls a similar transformation in *St. Vincent*. Vincent is the quintessential cranky character, but eventually finds a small amount of satisfaction in befriending a young boy and his mother. Audiences don't often learn to love mean characters, but will usually end up giving a cranky character a chance.

Helping Hellraisers is a Worthy Cause

Murray has long realized he doesn't have to be the star of the show in order to steal the show. Many great stories walk us through the journey of a disruptive protagonist trying to find their way in the world. BM has recognized that the character that helps that protagonist find their way becomes instantly lovable to audiences. In *Rushmore*, Murray's Herman Blume helps Max Fischer with every project the boy can dream up. In the process, we end up loving Murray for it. In *Lost in Translation*, he walks beside Charlotte through her "lostness" without ever using her weakness to his advantage. As a result, we are so thankful for the Bill Murrays in our own lives. Characters who must face internal maturity or change over the course of the story usually need a catalyst, in the form of a person, to accomplish such a feat. Murray understands the need for subtlety that these characters require. We need these characters in our stories, and we need them in real life.

Tenacity Tickles Audiences

We can't help it. We love to see a character persevere until they reach their goal. Just like in dramas, the more difficult the situation a comedic character finds themselves in, the more we like it. Watching Murray face impossible odds never gets old. But this method doesn't just work because we're watching Bill Murray. It works because it's good storytelling. It can work in your story too. In *Groundhog Day*, we watch BM wake up to the same impossible situation everyday. How will he ever stop the cycle? The solution to the problem in the story is not nearly as satisfying as the process we experience with Murray in trying over and over again, eventually embracing his situation, and then finally learning the secret to overcoming the insufferable. In *Quick Change*, Murray's character has a simple goal – get to the airport. The comedy doesn't lie in how many obstacles lie between Murray and the airport. The comedy lies in Murray's reaction to each obstacle and his ability to somehow keep trying without giving up. We love to see our hero win in a story. We will empathize when they don't. But we insist that they try with all their might.

Cocky Characters Are Fun, But Still Must Learn Lessons

We've all wished for just the right zinger to sling at the person who cuts us off in traffic. People who always have something clever to say intrigue us. We occasionally want to be them. But we also recognize the need for these folks to be put in their place. Bill Murray understands this. He makes us laugh by allowing his confidence to exceed his abilities. But he also keeps us on his side when he inevitably must be humbled. Well-written characters will do the same. In *Ghostbusters*, Murray's Dr. Peter Venkman always has a clever word at the ready. His comical dressing down of his fellow Ghostbusters for their glaring shortcomings makes us snicker. But the real laughs come when we see Venkman slimmed in goo by a ghost. We know the universe has balanced when BM is taken down a notch, where we can continue to root for him. In *Stripes*, Murray goes from taxi-driving smart-ass to the army's funniest soldier, but the story only works because his drill sergeant puts him in his place whenever the character's swagger bumps into his barrack mates.

STRENGTH IN WEAKNESS:
5 FLAWS THAT CAN ACTUALLY MAKE YOUR
CHARACTER STRONGER

When we create characters, we're often looking to
add qualities that make them strong or interesting.
However, asking where your character is weak can be
an even greater way to make a protagonist compelling.
A character's weakness should cloud their better
judgment. It should cause them to take actions they
might not normally take. Here are five flaws that can
actually strengthen your character.

A Weakness for Family

A staple of mob stories and gangster epics has become
to make the hardened criminal a big softie when it
comes to his family. We've seen this in the *Godfather*
trilogy, *The Sopranos*, and most recently in *Black
Mass*. Jimmy "Whitey" Bulger has a heart of stone
when it comes to everyone on the planet, except his
mother and his son. When these people mean so
much to a character like Jimmy, we know the biggest
conflict we can create will be to take them away from
him. This same weakness allows Solomon Northup to
endure unspeakable pain in *12 Years A Slave*. His wife
means more to him than anything. When she is taken
away, his weakness for her drives the rest of the film's
storyline.

Even comedic characters fall for the weakness of
family. Daniel Hillard takes on the personae of an old
British nannie in *Mrs. Doubtfire*, just so he can be
around his children. The weakness of family works as
a story element because so many of us can relate to its

power.

A Weakness for Love

Most of us have made a poor decision motivated by matters of the heart. Love can cause us to betray all reason, go on dangerous adventures, and sacrifice all we have spent years building. In *The American President*, Andrew Shepherd risks the prestige of the most powerful position in the world, just so he can pursue a woman who captures his interest and eventually his heart. Lloyd Christmas leaves all he knows and loves to travel across the country to return a brief case to a woman he fell in love with instantly in *Dumb and Dumber*. And in *Pretty Woman*, Edward Lewis gives up his reputation, money, and long-time business partner to be with a woman of ill repute. No one ever faults the lengths a character is willing to go to in a story for love. We all understand and may have been there ourselves.

A Weakness for Acceptance

It's the thing that drives us to cheer on a playground bully even when we know how wrong he is – acceptance. Our need to feel admired, revered, or even just a part of the group can drive us to the edges of sanity. In *Whiplash*, Andrew is literally willing to lay down his life and relationships to gain the respect of a prolific teacher. William Miller leaves his life, home, and family to pursue the acceptance of the coolest rock stars on the planet in *Almost Famous*. But the lengths Max Fischer is willing to go to in *Rushmore*, in order to be seen and accepted, sets a standard few characters can live up to. The lesson and theme in nearly all stories of this sort is that we must first learn to accept ourselves before anyone else will consider that an option.

A Weakness for the Truth

A search for the truth has been the driving force of many great characters over the centuries of storytelling. Those who are willing to sacrifice in order to see and say things as they are will always gain the respect of the audience. In *Dead Poets Society*, John Keating is willing to lose his prestigious job in order to declare the truth before young men who will be forever impacted by his bravery. Truman Burbank gives up literally everything in his world in order to know who he really is and the truth about his environment in *The Truman Show*. Martin Sixsmith is so driven by the truth surrounding his new friend's child; he gives up the harshest part of his own identity in *Philomena*. Jack Nicholson famously uttered that we can't handle the truth in *A Few Good Men*, but that will never keep us from going after it, and holding those who do in great esteem.

A Weakness for Justice

Those who have stood up for justice throughout history have often paid a dear price. Some of the most moving stories ever told center on people who laid down their lives in order to speak up against laws, systems, and individuals who would deny equality to all peoples. Kate Macer puts her life on the line day after day in an attempt to stop evil drug cartels that murder and destabilize innocent people in Mexico in *Sicario*. Using photos on the wall of a pizzeria as a metaphor for a much larger injustice, Mookie battles against a system that has refused to recognize African Americans in *Do The Right Thing*. In one of the most iconic roles of all time, Jefferson Smith stands up for the little guy until he collapses on the floor of Congress in *Mr. Smith Goes to Washington*. Seeing those who would defend the powerless in a society and people falsely accused empowers us to stand against the injustices, both small and great, that we see in our own lives.

NAKED AND AFRAID:
6 THINGS YOUR CHARACTER SHOULD FEAR

There are a few base emotions that have driven human beings since we've had any form of consciousness. Most important to our survival has been *fear*. We won't last long on this planet if we don't learn to run from things that threaten our existence. One goal of good writing is to construct characters that feel as human as we do. The most well designed characters respond the same way we would. They rejoice when we would rejoice. They cry when we would cry. And they are afraid when we would be afraid. Here are six things your character should tremble at the thought of.

Losing What They Love

Most of us can handle whatever comes our way, as long as it only affects us. Our weakness shows when trouble hits those we love. Determining what (or who) your character loves before you begin telling your story is essential. Knowing what they love will also revel their weakness. Sure, we can pitch our heroines against the most powerful forces in the universe and that can be exciting. However, the audience may or may not care. Audiences tend to invest more deeply when a character is fighting for someone else – when we can sense that they are afraid of losing something they love.

In *Carol*, the protagonist is afraid of losing her daughter, who she adores more than anything, if she gives in to her feelings for Therese Belivet. Over the course of the story, Carol must choose between living an authentic life and losing what she cares

about most. We can relate to the difficulty of such a
choice. In *Mrs. Doubtfire*, Daniel Hillard is also afraid
of losing his children. These stories work because we
know how people feel about their kids. The thought of
losing them is the worst thing many members of the
audience can imagine.

Being Left Alone

There is a moment in the 1985 film, *Young Sherlock
Holmes*, when Holmes is asked what he wants to be
when he grows up. He looks across the courtyard, sees
his girlfriend and replies, "I wish never to be alone."
Just as with losing a child, the fear of being alone is
one of the oldest, most base fears we experience as
humans. Even the staunchest introverts need people.
Films such as *As Good As It Gets* play up this tension
as the central conflict in the film. Most romantic
comedies have the fear of being left alone at their core.
The 40 Year Old Virgin revolves around this theme.
The central characters in *Almost Famous*, *American
Beauty*, and even *It's A Wonderful Life* all struggle with
this fear.

Not Achieving Their Goal

Many people derive their worth from their work.
What they accomplish in life professionally or in the
arena they love seems to define who they are. Many
characters are driven by the same desire. In life, we
often have so many goals that our existence becomes
confusing. We are comforted to see a character on
screen that has one singular goal that will complete
them. We long for the same. In *Creed*, Donny Johnson
fears he will be seen as a punch line if he doesn't

accomplish his goal. He becomes willing to do *anything* to keep this from happening. Many sports stories revolve around this fear. *The Karate Kid*, *Friday Night Lights*, and *Million Dollar Baby* are just a few. Of course, fear works in every genre. In *Misery*, Paul Sheldon's fear that he won't be able to achieve his goal by escaping Annie Wilkes becomes so visceral that we find ourselves clenching the arms of our chair, taking on the fear as our own.

Being Naked (Or Revealed)

It's a common feeling. A person gets a new job and fears they will be "revealed" as a fraud and unqualified for the position when they first begin. Sometimes these fears play out in dreams where we show up at school or some other social function naked. Many of us experience great anxiety about being seen for who we truly are. We go to great lengths to avoid these revelations.

In *Spotlight*, Robby Robinson ironically works to reveal corruption while simultaneously being afraid his own shortcomings will be seen. In *Brooklyn*, Ellis has her friends teach her how to eat spaghetti without making a mess, because she fears she will be seen as unfamiliar with the Italian culture of her boyfriend's family. Sometimes, however, the stakes are much higher than spaghetti. Josie Geller fears blowing her cover at the high school she is writing about in *Never Been Kissed*. And in *The Departed*, Billy spends the entire film trying to avoid being revealed to the crime family he works for, fearing it will cost him his life.

Having to Live with their Mistakes

Our pasts have a way of catching up with us. At least
we fear this to be true. We all fear having to live with
the mistakes we have made. We know that mistakes
will be unavoidable. We hope the consequences of
these mistakes will be short lived. *A History of Violence*
centers on having to deal with the mistakes of one's
past. In *Secret in Their Eyes*, Ray spends the course
of the story trying to atone for not meeting a friend at
a bakery – a decision that might have cost her life. He
feels if he can bring her killer to justice, he won't have
to live with his mistake. The driving tension of the
story is the fear that he will. *Schindler's List*, *Shame*,
and *Unforgiven* all feature characters dealing with the
fear of having to live with their mistakes.

Not Being Worthy

We've all felt like we weren't good enough. At times, we
feel like we aren't good enough for our spouse. Other
times, we feel unworthy of an opportunity. Deep down,
we hold fear about our value and worth. This causes
one of the greatest epidemics the world today faces –
insecurity. When we feel insecure, we say things we
wish we hadn't. We do things we regret. We present
a version of ourselves that is inauthentic. Great
characters are no different.

Even after escaping *Room*, Ma fears she is unworthy
of her child and her new life. In *Trainwreck*, Amy fears
she is unworthy of a healthy relationship. Sam fears
she is unworthy to be president of the house in *Dear
White People*. And Cady fears she is unworthy to sit
with the "cool girls" in the lunchroom in *Mean Girls*.

We relate to all these scenarios because we too fear we may not be worthy. Someone once said the best stories are actually psychotherapy. We experience this when we see a character overcome their insecurities. If they find themselves to be worthy, then maybe, just maybe – there is hope for us.

6 GHOSTS THAT GRANT BETTER STORIES

Writers sometimes mistakenly ghettoize ghosts solely to the realm of horror films. It's easy to forget that the ghost takes many forms and can work in any genre at any time of the year. Here are six ghosts, both literal and figurative, that can improve any story.

The Ghost of Revelation

The ghost of revelation appears when a character has a secret or an issue they have avoided dealing with. It can come in the form of a person who stands as a reminder for the issue, an image or symbol that brings up memories, or an unexpected event that forces the issue to the forefront of the character's life. Ghosts of revelation demand to be revealed. They fight to get out of the closet. They will continue to plague our character until she relents and eventually surrenders or is defeated. In *The Silence of the Lambs*, Hannibal Lecter eventually forces Clarice Starling to reveal her ghost. In *A History of Violence*, Tom Stall's ghost shows up in the form of Carl Fogarty, who has come to reveal Tom's past. In *Election,* the ghost of what Jim McAllister has done demands to be revealed and provides the central conflict in the story, while in turn ruining his life.

The Family Ghost

Perhaps the most common ghost in storytelling is the family ghost. This ghost represents either the death of a family member earlier in our character's life or sometimes just the absence of that family member. The unifying factor for all family ghosts is the pain they bring. Batman is constantly haunted by the ghosts of his dead parents, as is Superman. Maximus carries a similar weight about his wife and son in *Gladiator.* Ray Charles is haunted by his role in his brother's death in *Ray.* *Cinderella* mourns both her mother and father. Max seems daily motivated by the loss of his mother in *Rushmore.* Elliot is lost over the loss of his father, who isn't dead but is absent, in E.T. Even in *Star Wars: A New Hope,* Luke Skywalker only agrees to go on his adventure after the death of his Aunt and Uncle.

The Tour Guide Ghost

Tour guide ghosts may be seen or unseen while navigating us through our story. Mostly, stories with tour guide ghosts are narrated by a ghost who leads us through the events that lead to their death. *American Beauty* and *Sunset Boulevard* are two of the most popular examples of this type of storytelling. However, *American History X, Looper, The Lovely Bones, Sin City, Warm Bodies, Watchmen,* and even *A Christmas Carol* all feature ghosts who walk us through the journey in one way or another.

The Possessive Ghost

The possessive ghost is an actual ghost that feels ownership of a person, place, or thing. In many of the oldest ghost stories, a ghost felt ownership over a house they once lived in and demanded they remain the sole occupant. They try to scare the new occupants away, of course, by haunting the house throughout the story. Some times, it's a person's body they feel ownership over and other times it might be a single object that once belonged to them. While films such as *Poltergeist* are classic examples of possessive ghost stories, *Field of Dreams* would also qualify as the baseball-playing ghosts feel a sense of ownership over the field they play on.

The Inconvenient Ghost

Inconvenient ghosts are rarely the main character in a story. Instead, they posses the unique ability to show up in our main character's life at moments most inopportune. Sometimes, it is to warn the main character about something. Some times it is to tell them something they need to hear. Other times, it's simply to be an annoyance. In the rare moment when the main character is the inconvenient ghost, the scenario usually plays out like the humorous exchange between Sam Wheat and Oda Mae Brown in *Ghost*. Obi Wan Kenobi shows up in *The Empire Strikes Back* to give Luke Skywalker some advice he'd rather not hear. This season of HBO's *The Leftovers* has Patti Levin showing back up at inopportune moments in Kevin Garvey's life. And the beloved *Beetlejuice* is perhaps the most entertaining inconvenient ghost of all time.

The Ghost of Achilles

Even the toughest characters usually have a soft spot. Giving a "Grade A Badass" a weakness can endear them to audiences in powerful ways. For Tony Soprano, it was his family. In *Citizen Kane*, Charles Foster Kane pines for his Rosebud. In *Mystic River*, Jimmy Markum is inconsolable whenever his daughter is mentioned. P.L. Travers is Teflon about everything in her life, except her father, whom her most famous work is based on in *Saving Mr. Banks*. Even good-natured Sean Maguire loses his cool as a counselor when Will Hunting disrespects his dead wife – she's clearly his Achilles ghost. The execution of a good Ghost of Achilles takes a bit up set up early on in the story to pay off effectively, but the results are usually well worth the effort.

GET A JOB!
6 WAYS TO USE YOUR CHARACTER'S
OCCUPATION TO DEVELOP YOUR STORY

In the United States, people often feel defined by what they do for a living. In the world of story, a character's occupation can have similar importance. If your character is of working age, audiences mostly expect to learn how they make their living. This may or may not be a significant element of the story. A character's occupation can, however, play an important role in the development of the overall narrative. Here are six ways to connect a character's job with the story you are creating around him or her.

The Job as Conflict

The most direct way to deal with your character's occupation is to make that job the central conflict in the story. In *42*, it's Jackie Robinson's job to play professional baseball. This job is the source of conflict between all the opponents he faces and himself. In *Dallas Buyer's Club*, Ron Woodruff creates a job selling medication to AIDS patients. This job becomes the central point of conflict in the story. *The Help*, *Belle*, and *Gravity* all feature key characters whose job is the conflict in the film.

The Job as Environment or
Setting for the Conflict

Every person who has ever held a job has experienced conflict in that job. This is likely why jobs make good environments and settings to explore our character's conflict. In *Moneyball*, Baseball is the environment the characters work in and thus the environment the conflict inhabits. In *High Fidelity*, it's the record shop that our protagonist lives and works in. In *Adventureland*, it's the theme park. *Field of Dreams*, *The 40 Year Old Virgin*, and even *The Godfather* all feature occupational environments key to the protagonist's development in the story.

The Job as Solution to the Conflict

Some of the most interesting characters ever developed have been those who make their living by solving conflicts. We love these characters because we all long for someone to help solve our own dilemmas. Austin Powers, James Bond, Sherlock Holmes, and Indiana Jones all have made occupations out of solving problems and mysteries no one else could solve. *Inherent Vice*, *Argo*, *Angels and Demons*, and *Ghostbusters* all feature characters who solve conflicts for a living, and who live to solve conflicts.

The Job as Winning

A staple among sports films, sometimes a character's job is simply to win. *The Karate Kid* was a student and didn't really have a job, except to win the karate tournament. Beatrice was an assassin, but her true task came to be winning by *Kill*(ing) *Bill*. The Permian High Panthers had no other job but to win in *Friday Night Lights*. It's safe to say the job of the protagonist in the upcoming *Creed* will be the same.

The Job as Survival of the Institution

Some characters don't have occupations either

because they are students and do not yet have a job or they are guests of institutions. Ferris has no job but to survive the institution of school in *Ferris Bueller's Day Off*. All the main characters in *The Breakfast Club* have the same job. The men in *The Shawshank Redemption* and *Cool Hand Luke* have the same "job" as well. All these characters primary occupation becomes simply surviving the institution of which they are part.

What Job? I'm on Vacation!

Occasionally in the world of story, we encounter characters who are either unemployed or on vacation. Even though his occupation is referenced, Clarke Griswold is clearly on *Vacation*. *Forgetting Sarah Marshall* features a protagonist on a vacation with a hidden agenda. *The Hangover* tells the story of a vacation (in the form of a bachelor's party) gone wrong. In *Couples' Retreat*, we meet a group of people all on vacation. Even *The Wizard of Oz* could be considered a vacation story since it features a character that is away from her normal life and tasks.

While the occupation of your character can be extremely important, it's key to not let that completely define them. Characters tend to fall flat when all we know of them is what they do to make money. Remember, just as none of us can be completely encompassed by our job descriptions, the same is true of the characters we create. Create well-rounded people, who have many layers, and a variety of interests. Then, their occupation becomes a lens to who they are instead of a singular definition.

LESSONS FROM BLACK WRITERS:
A LOOK AT THE 7 MEN AND WOMEN
NOMINATED FOR ACADEMY AWARDS

2016 is remembered as a year when racial diversity highlighted the conversation. Screenwriting is also an area where few people of color have seen their work recognized throughout history. Only two African Americans have ever won the award for adapted screenplay and no one has ever taken home the big prize for an original screenplay. It is also notable that only one black woman has ever been nominated and that was more than 40 years ago. Here's a look at the seven black writers who have been nominated for Academy Awards in the writing categories, the stories they brought to the screen, and the lessons we can learn from their work.

Suzanne de Passe
Nominated for Original Screenplay
Lady Sings the Blues (1972)

In 1972, black writers saw their first glimmer of hope, with nominations in both the adapted and original categories. De Passe's story about jazz legend Billie Holliday, starred Diana Ross in the leading role. The script follows Holiday's tragic beginnings as a housekeeper in a Baltimore brothel, where she was repeatedly raped, through her rise to stardom. The script is an unflinching look at a complicated woman's genius as well as her demons, which led to her premature death at the age of 44. If there's one lesson we can take from this wonderfully complex storytelling, it is that powerful stories must show a protagonist's greatest weaknesses as well as their strengths. It is

in Holliday's humanity that we see beauty. It takes
bravery to show the shadow of a beloved character.
This is exactly what Suzanne de Passe did in this story
and the Academy rightfully acknowledged her for it.
De passe continues to work in film and television and
presently is developing an MLK film alongside Steven
Spielberg.

Lonne Elder
Nominated for Adapted Screenplay
Sounder (1972)

The pressure of taking a well-loved book and adapting
it for the screen can be unnerving. *Sounder* tells of a
young boy's journey to visit his father, who has been
convicted of a petty crime, in a prison camp for black
sharecroppers in 1933. The film starred Cicely Tyson,
Paul Winfield and Kevin Hooks. Elder initially refused
the assignment of working on the film, afraid the story
would be more sympathetic to the dog at the center of
the tale, than the people who cared for him. Director
Martin Ritt eventually convinced Elder to come on
board saying, "I wanted to keep *Sounder* accurate in
its historical context and not go off on any present-
day fantasies." Writers today would do well to examine
Elder's masterful balance of the horrors of racism and
the universal theme of family importance. One word
that appears time and again from those discussing the
film is *honesty*. If audiences sense a writer's view of
the world is anything less than honest, they will reject
their story outright. Elder knew this and kept this
principle central to his writing. He scripted a sequel
to *Sounder* a few years later and continued to write
stories about the black experience until his death in
1996 at the age of 68.

Charles Fuller
Nominated for Adapted Screenplay
A Soldier's Story (1984)

It would be over a decade before another black writer
would be nominated after the successes of de Passe
and Edler. Finally, in 1984, Charles Fuller brought
the story of a military murder investigation involving
black soldiers to the screen. The script was based on
Fuller's own stage work, *A Soldier's Play*, and took
loose inspiration from Herman Melville's novella, *Billy
Budd*. Fuller tackled the difficult theme of anger and
resentment in the Black community toward those who
find success in arenas historically controlled by white
men. He discussed his use of storytelling as a means
for change in a 1982 interview, stating, "To spend
one's life being angry, and in the process doing nothing
to change it, is to me ridiculous. I could be mad all
day long, but if I'm not doing a damn thing, what
difference does it make?" The protagonist in Fuller's
story, Captain Richard Davenport, is compelling to the
audience but disliked by everyone around him. There
is an important lesson to be learned here. Everyone
in your story can despise your protagonist, but it is
the job of the writer to make the audience empathetic.
This can be no easy task, but Fuller accomplishes it
brilliantly. Charles Fuller continues to write stories
and remains active with the Writers Guild of America
East.

Spike Lee
Nominated for Original Screenplay
Do the Right Thing (1989)

Some film historians have commented that *Do the*

Right Thing's loss to *Rain Man* for Best Original Screenplay in 1989 is one of cinema's greatest travesties. Lee's examination of modern racism, justice, and anger was deemed "culturally significant" by the Library of Congress in 1999 and was added to the National Film Registry that same year, one of only six films to receive the honor in their first year of eligibility. The script takes place in a single day, the hottest of the summer in Brooklyn. It features a host of neighborhood characters intersecting around a single catalyst -- there are no pictures of black celebrities on the wall of the local Italian pizzeria.

The narrative methodically unfolds, showing how the effect of this discovery eventually turns into a neighborhood riot, where businesses and even lives are lost. Lee makes a daring move at the end of his script. His protagonist's action will upset some of his audience, but that is true to who that character is. He demonstrates one of the most key, yet difficult, principles screenwriting. Characters must do what *they* would do in a given situation, not what the *writer* would do. It can take years before a writer can even tell the difference. However, only when we can parse out the nuances between ourselves and our characters will our stories begin to possess power. Lee's latest film, *Chiraq*, was released in 2015.

John Singleton
Nominated for Original Screenplay
Boyz n the Hood (1991)

1991 was the last time a Black writer was nominated for Best Original Screenplay. While Spike Lee had brought the modern Black experience in New York

City to the screen in 1989, John Singleton would show
audiences what life in Los Angeles was like for Black
men and women. *Boyz n the Hood* provided a portal
into the realities and dangers of inner city life for many
white Americans. Singleton defied the stereotypes
about Black youths and presented a story about
family, humanity, and the myth of redemptive violence.
While Cuba Gooding Jr.'s portrayal of the protagonist,
Tre, would make him a breakout star, it would be the
secondary characters that would steal the show.

Tre's best friend, Ricky, and Ricky's brother,
Doughboy, the first role ever played by Ice Cube,
would provide the heart of the story. Many writers
focus all their story energy on their protagonist, whose
importance can not be underestimated. However, the
protagonist cannot accomplish everything a story
needs. Secondary characters can provide elements
in a story that truly make the script what it is. John
Singleton went on to great success and continues to
write and direct significant work for the screen.

Geoffrey Fletcher
Won for Adapted Screenplay
Precious (2009)

Finally, in 2009, a Black writer would not only be
nominated for a writing award by the Academy, but
would win. *Precious*, based on the novel *Push* by
Sapphire, tells the story of an illiterate 16-year-old girl
living in Harlem with her abusive mother. The end of
the script is especially moving as the protagonist has
developed and learned important skills for her journey.
However, the narrative remains nuanced and does not
lead the character into unrealistic waters. Fletcher

captures the heartache of the situation without ever pandering to the character or the audience. He guides the protagonist through her journey and even manages to teach the audience something about tenacity and hope. One of the key elements that makes *Precious* unique is that it is a story of a character we had never seen before. As writers, we should constantly be searching to tell the tales of characters unfamiliar to the audience. At the very least, we must figure out methods of telling new stories about characters that audiences have been long familiar with. Geoffrey Fletcher continues to be an important voice in American screenwriting while teaching at Columbia University and NYU.

John Ridley
Won for Adapted Screenplay
12 Years a Slave (2013)

Based on Solomon Northup's 1853 memoir, *12 Years a Slave* marked the first time a Black writer would craft the script for a film that won the Best Picture award. Telling the story of a New York State-born free African American who was kidnapped and sold into slavery, Ridley developed themes that remain as relevant today as they were when the original story was told. Many critics noted how the story never shied away from the brutality of slavery and those who profited by it. This is important for screenwriters. Shying away from the difficult or brutal aspects of a story will never lead to connection with the audience. While all writers desire success, it's important to remember that not every script we write will be for every audience and not every audience will be right for every script. We must stay with the stories that live inside us and never look away from all the warts and ugliness they wear. John Ridley continues to write for film and television. His most recent work can be seen in the TV series, *American Crime*. His latest adaptation for the big screen, *Ben-Hur*, was released in 2016.

LIQUID STORYTELLING:
8 WAYS TO USE WATER IN YOUR SCRIPT

Few elements used in storytelling have a longer legacy than water. Every early mythic tradition tells of a great flood and humankind's battle to overcome those uncontrollable forces of nature. People for millennia crafted stories to explain why water fell from the sky, from cliffs, and from their own eyes. Water is said to symbolize the subconscious in everything from dreams to filmmaking. It can be a literal underworld that we continue to try to explore and understand. Dating back to times when tales were told around fires, storytellers have understood that there is something universal in using natural elements such as earth, fire, wind, and water in their narratives. Today's stories are no different. Water remains an element with unlimited uses in holding the attention of an audience. Here are eight ways to use water to improve your storytelling.

Conflict

It's no secret that having a scene take place in the rain makes it more dramatic. Even seeing a character soaking wet paints a picture of the conflict the character is experiencing – think Brando's famous "Stella!" scene from *A Streetcar Named Desire*. Toby Maguire and Kirsten Dunst shared a memorable kiss in *Spiderman*. The rain that pours down in this scene is an unmistakable symbol of the complex conflict Peter Parker experiences in that moment. Rain is often used in competitive sports movies to increase the clash as well as action films and thrillers like the *Jurassic Park* series.

Hope

Rain is not exclusive used to represent conflict,
however. It can also be used to symbolize hope. Andy
Dufresne claims to crawl through "a river of shit"
to escape in *The Shawshank Redemption*. When he
finally exits the sewer pipe, which was his salvation,
He stands and raises both hands into the sky while
the rain pours down on him. The sky unleashes a
cleansing mix of redemption and hope for the life
that now awaits him. *On Golden Pond* uses water to
symbolize the unifying hope that the Thayer family
so desperately needs. Having drifted apart through
distance and strife, the unchanging water that
surrounds them becomes a symbol of the future that
awaits them at the end of the story.

Cleansing

Horror films feature an inordinate number of scenes
that take place in showers and bathtubs. Besides
being an expected trope, and perhaps an excuse to
feature some nudity, showers and tubs represent an
oft-used theme of the horror genre - cleansing. The
idea of washing away the dirt that has been collected
through our actions has appealed to storytellers
throughout the ages. Scenes in showers are often
followed by moments where the vulnerable are
punished, suggesting that there will be no redemption
for the sin committed by the character. The shower
scene is *Psycho* has become a cultural icon but even
films at the opposite end of the spectrum use the same
device. *Pretty Woman* offers a moment where the two
lead characters bathe together, cleansing themselves
of the past faults they both have indulged. However,

the scene is also a pre-cursor to the deep valley their relationship is about to enter.

Resurrection

Occasionally, the cleansing a character experiences is a literal baptism, meant to offer a new life. Just as is symbolized in the baptism, the character is submerged in water and dies a death to their old self, then emerges a new creation. Karl Childers experiences this in *Sling Blade* as does Delmar O'Donnell in *O Brother, Where Art Thou?* In other films, such as *The Matrix*, there is a figurative resurrection, as when Neo emerges from a water-like liquid.

Punishment

Water also can serve as a severe punishment in a story. The Dude experiences a comic yet horrific "swirlie" in his own toilet in *The Big Lebowski*. In *Castaway*, Chuck Noland feels punished by the unforgiving water that surrounds the island that has become his home. And in *Les Misrables*, Javert casts himself into the Seine River as his own punishment, unable to accept the grace of Jean Valjean.

Location

While water can represent many things in a story, it can also serve as a major location for where the story takes place – which may or may not include symbolism. *The Finest Hours* and *In The Heart of the Sea* both take place mainly in ocean waters. *Finding Nemo, Titanic, The Perfect Storm,* and *20,000 Leagues Under the Sea* greatly share this location as well. And while they don't necessarily take place *in* the water, *On the Waterfront*, *Pirates of the Caribbean* and *Jaws* all certainly take place *around* the water. Other films such as *Everest* take place on and in snow and ice.

Necessity

We must also remember that water is a basic necessity for our survival. Most of us share a negative quality with characters we see on the screen – we don't drink enough water. We are reminded of this fluid necessity when we see Finn share a watering hole with a creature in *Star Wars: The Force Awakens* or the desperation for the control of water in *Mad Max: Fury Road* and *Chinatown*. Water makes multiple appearances in *The Goonies*, perhaps most memorably when the Goonies are offered water by Mama Fratelli. *The Revenant* also uses water as a story device as is seen with a certain drinking canteen, not too mention a flowing river in the final scene of the story.

Separation

One of the most heart-breaking ways water can be used in storytelling is to keep people apart. Families seem to know no greater pain than when separated by large expanses of water. We feel Ellis's pain in *Brooklyn*, knowing how detached she senses she is from her family back in Ireland. Cinque voices the cry of separation all enslaved Africans feel by the ocean that lies between them and their home in *Amistad*. The more vast and insurmountable the body of water, the greater anguish a character will experience.

9 CLOCKS FOR YOUR HERO TO RACE AGAINST

Conflict is a necessity in good storytelling. One of the strongest ways you can increase the conflict in your story is to compress time. There's perhaps no greater thrill for an audience than watching a character race against a merciless clock. Here are nine clocks to challenge your hero with.

The Blind Clock

You know it's coming but can't see WHEN it's coming. Many powerful stories have been structured around impending doom – a natural disaster, a historical event, and the list goes on. We know when the clock strikes the appointed time, the rug will be pulled from underneath our hero. We just can't SEE the clock. We don't know how close that appointed time is. *San Andreas*, *Twister*, and *Titanic* all center around blind clocks.

The Seasonal Clock

A seasonal clock ticks down to the end of a season or era. In these stories, our protagonist must accomplish their goal before winter hits or perhaps before summer arrives and the school year is over. These devices are often used in stories that take place in schools or the lives of teenagers. Whether it's finding a date before prom or asking a boy out before school is dismissed for the summer, the stakes always seem high when every day moves our character one step closer to their last chance. A number of John Hughes's movies are structured around seasonal clocks. *American Pie* is another example -- where a group of boys make a pact to lose their virginity by prom night.

The Revelation Clock

Sometimes, our character is hiding a secret and their story is structured around the difficulty they are having in keeping that secret. They often have a goal they must accomplish before they are found out. The revelation clock transcends all genres and is one of the most used, albeit effective, devices in storytelling. The protagonists in *Never Been Kissed, Mrs. Doubtfire, She's The Man,* and *Tootsie* all try to accomplish their goals before their true identity is revealed. In films such as *The Wolf of Wall Street* and *Blow,* the protagonists are attempting to complete goals before their crimes come to light.

The Event Clock

The event clock is winding down to the third act in the story when the big game/fight/contest or similar event will occur. Our hero has often spent the entire second act training and overcoming obstacles to get here, and now it's time to see if all they've endured was worth it. Event clocks are common in films that revolve around athletes or sports teams as in *The Karate Kid* or *Friday Night Lights.* They are also seen in comedies such as *Pitch Perfect, Birdman,* and *School of Rock.* One of the most popular event clocks remains the wedding clock. We see this used in *Bridesmaids, My Best Friend's Wedding, My Big Fat Greek Wedding, The Wedding Singer, Coming to America,* and even *The Hangover.*

The Treasure Clock

Our protagonist has a very clear goal – to get the treasure. But their enemy is also after the same treasure. The treasure clock ticks in the race to get there before the enemy does. While mainly a staple of action/adventure films like the *Indiana Jones* movies, *The Goonies*, and *National Treasure*, we also see this clock in stories like *O Brother Where Art Thou?*

The Enemy's Clock

Many heroes are saviors racing against the clock before their enemy has an opportunity to enact their plan. We've seen Clarice Starling desperately trying to catch Buffalo Bill before he can kill his next victim in *Silence of the Lambs*. We've seen Tony Stark and his *Avengers* try to stop Ultron from realizing his plan. We've even seen a construction worker trying to stop an evil tyrant from gluing the Lego universe together permanently in *The Lego Movie*. All are heroes fighting against the moment when their antagonist will accomplish his or her goal.

The Monster Clock

The goal of the hero in a story running the monster clock is usually just to escape. These films leave audiences biting their nails and plotting escape plans for the character they're watching on screen. We just want to see them get away before the monster gets them. While these clocks are most often found in horror films, *Jurassic Park* and *Jurassic World* take great advantage of this device. Chase movies, like *Mad Max: Fury Road* and the upcoming *Pixels*, rely on the same sort of clock.

The Deadline Clock

Sometimes, our hero faces an immovable deadline.
There is nothing they can do to change it. In *Back
to the Future*, Marty McFly must unite his parents
before lightening strikes the clock tower, which is his
only shot at returning home to the life he knows. The
climax of the film features a literal ticking clock. Will
Ferrell's character must *Get Hard* before his upcoming
prison sentence. In *Brewster's Millions*, Monty
Brewster must spend 30 million dollars in 30 days
without acquiring any assets or giving the money away
in order to collect his full inheritance.

The Sanity Clock

Stories that use the sanity clock challenge our
protagonist to simply survive before losing their
wits. These stories are often about humanity's battle
against institutions. *The Shawshank Redemption*, *One
Flew Over the Cuckoos Nest*, *American Beauty*, and
Neighbors all have heroes (of sorts) battling against
sands in an hourglass of sanity. When the sand
runs out – which will always happen in these stories
-- drastic measures will be taken by or against the
protagonist. In other words, this is when the fun starts
(or ends).

WRITING THE FEUDIAN TRIO:
10 EXAMPLES OF THE TRIFECTA OF CHARACTER
DESIGN IN STORYTELLING

Sigmund Feud is credited for popularizing the idea that the human psyche is multi-faceted. He suggested that our personalities could be seen as having three parts: the id, the ego and the superego. Long before Freud's suggestion of this idea, stories were often told with a key character representing one of these three aspects of the psyche. The conflict engaged by these three ideas running into each other gives us more than enough drama to keep a story fresh for two hours of screen time, which is why this design is often seen in screenplays.

For anyone who missed the day they discussed Freud's ideas in school, the id is the primal component of the personality. Experts attribute uncoordinated instinctual trends to the id. Our aggression to fight against death or harm, our libido or instinct towards sex, hunger, and thirst are all aspects of the id. The ego is the mediator between our sometimes unrealistic id and our over-idealistic superego. The ego is rational and oriented toward problem solving. Feud used this example. The id is like a horse and the ego is the rider on top of that horse. The superego consists of the conscious and the ideal self. Rather than just mediating, the superego can actually stop the id from doing certain things it may incline us to do. In case you are still a little confused, here are ten films that use characters to represent the id, the ego and the superego in their story structure.

The Nice Guys

Jackson Healy, portrayed by Russell Crowe, represents the id in the new Shane Black comedy. He goes into every situation swinging. He embodies all our human base instincts. Ryan Gosling plays Holland March, the ego in our story. He often mediates between Crowe's id instincts and the idealistic approach his daughter, Holly. Speaking of Holly, she is the superego of the story. She shows her power by literally stopping the id of Crowe from killing a man, near the end of the film.

The Dark Knight

The id in *The Dark Knight* is The Joker. He appeals to the primal side of humanity with his philosophical approach in society. Bruce Wayne/Batman is the ego trying to mediate between The Joker's id and the idealistic views of society, specifically Commissioner Gordon and Harvey Dent. Dent best personifies the superego, with his desire to take the moral high ground above the chaos.

Ferris Bueller's Day Off

Ferris is the highly entertaining id of this story. He is interested in whatever his instincts push him towards, as long as it's pleasurable and fun. Cameron is the superego, reluctant about any pleasure that might be less than ideal or moral. Ferris's girlfriend, Sloane, is the ego, mediating the extremes, and providing level-headed balance.

The Matrix

Neo represents the id. Trinity is the superego. Morpheus is the ego. The film's plot is structured around the conflicts and balancing act that encircles the three.

Top Gun

The Tom Cruise classic has been in the news lately, because of its 25th anniversary. The story has endured greatly because of Maverick's id and Iceman's superego. Of course, Goose's ego is what many of us remember being the highlight of the film.

The Wizard Of Oz

The classic from Kansas is Freudian psychology 101. The id is The Tin Man, who represents the heart. The superego is The Scarecrow, representing the brain. And the ego is The Cowardly Lion, representing the courage it takes to mediate between the two.

The Breakfast Club

Proving the trio works across genres and generations, the John Hughes film plays out a Freudian character design with the males in the story. Bender is the id, who is loud, instinctual, and rebelling against authority. Andy is the superego, a jock who has strong ideals and tries to keep Bender in line. Brian, the ego, is the nice guy, mediating and attempting to reason between the others.

Harold And Kumar Go To Whitecastle

Harold plays the superego, highly moral about getting
the work done that he's been assigned. The id is Neil
Patrick Harris, a man absolutely consumed by his
own urges. Kumar is the ego, seeing the value in both
approaches and trying to create a third way.

Jaws

In this tale of a man trying to catch a fish, Quint is the
anger-prone id. Hooper is the idealistic superego. And
Brody is the ego mediating the Freudian feud.

The Lord Of The Rings

Tolkien was a master of psychological storytelling,
working in three different sets of Freudian trios to
the expanded universe of this story. Within the ring-
bearing trio, we have Gollum as the id, Frodo as the
ego, and Samwise as the superego. Within the hunters,
we have Gimli as the id, Aragorn as the ego, and
Legolas as the superego. And within the world of *The
Hobbit*, we have a Freudian trio among the wizards.
Radgast is the id. Gandalf is the ego. Saruman as the
superego.

10 WAYS TO TAKE A GREAT CHARACTER TO THE SCREEN

Some of the greatest films ever made have been character studies. Sure, there is a well-structured story sitting just below the surface that allows us to develop the character in meaningful and interesting ways. However, the purpose and driving force behind the story is to explore what it means to live inside someone else's skin which is another way to investigate what it means to be human. Far too many stories fail because they are based on a clever concept but feature paper-thin characters who lack any sort of dimension. One of the best methods for creating a powerful story is to begin with a juicy character. Some writers follow the discipline of writing ten pages about their protagonist and the character's backstory before they ever even begin the outlining or story development process. If you have an idea for a truly great character and believe that you sincerely understand who that person is, here are ten ways to take them into the plot of a powerful narrative.

The Bio

Certainly, one of the simplest ways to take a character you've developed to the screen is to use the elements from their biography to create the structure of your story. Your character's biography should include the most significant moments from their life. Taking one of these moments to create your entire plot from can make for a great story. A word of caution: this doesn't always work well. Many times there are things about the character that we need to know as a writer that we should never reveal to the audience. At most, we should only allude to them. *A Beautiful Mind* is one example of using a character's biography in order to develop the story around them.

The Backstory

The backstory is sometimes called the ghost. This is because it refers to a person or event in the character's past that still haunts them. Taking this person or event and crafting the entire plot around explaining the impact and exact details surrounding such can make for powerful storytelling. Remember, we don't need to understand *everything* that happened in a character's past to understand who they are. A good rule of thumb can be to tell us much more about much less. *A History of Violence* is an excellent example of this technique.

The Secret

If you have developed a character that will be engaging to your audience, one method that can expand who they are into a story is to give them a secret. It could be something they are ashamed of, such as a murder. It could also be something positive; perhaps the character hides their fortunes in order to make sure those who love them do so for the right reasons. *Coming to America* uses this method to great success.

The Weakness

Great characters will have an Achilles heel. Often, the entire plot of your story can be built around this. Sometimes the weakness will be a secret that no one else knows. Other times, the weakness is clearly

known to everyone and the character must bear
the burden of trying to succeed despite this. Even
characters as pure as Superman have their kryptonite.
Many times, a character's weakness is their family,
because this is so universally relatable. Aaron Paul's
character is a perfect example of someone with this
weakness on Hulu's *The Path*.

The Passion

Seeing a character really care about something is an
effective way to drive audiences toward empathizing
with them. Stories work best when our protagonist
really wants something. The plot can then center
around the lengths the character will go to get it.
Seeing Michael B. Jordan's passion for boxing in *Creed*
causes us to want to follow his story, wherever it goes.

The Question

A character's passion may lead them to a question
they cannot live without seeing answered. This
especially works well in adventure stories or tales
about detectives. However, this technique can also
work well across dramas. *Philomena* and *Woman
in Gold* are both stories about characters driven to
answer a singular question.

The Person

If you've built the bio for a truly interesting character,
we will know something about who they love and
would be willing to sacrifice for. Creating a story about
this character then having to fight for that love or
sacrifice for that person can be heart-warming and

even nerve-wracking. Katniss being willing to risk her own life so her sister will be spared is the catalyst for the entire *Hunger Games* series.

The Unexpected

One interesting exercise to put your character through is to ask, "What's the most unexpected thing that could happen to them?" Another way to set this scenario up is to ask "What's the worst thing that could happen to my unique character?" For example, if your character is a 60-year-old woman who has become a pizza delivery driver, but also owes money to the mob – who will be the one group she doesn't want to have to deliver a pizza to? Walking into a room, holding a pizza, only to face the people you've been trying to avoid, would be the last thing that character would expect. Having a sorority move in to the house next door while he's trying to sell his own home is the last thing Seth Rogen expects in *Neighbors 2*.

The Opportunity

If we know a character's passion, seeing them get the opportunity to put that passion to the test can be a powerful way to bring that character to the screen. Seeing an athlete have the opportunity to play in the big game, seeing the loser have the opportunity to go to the prom with the person of their dreams, and seeing the poor servant get the opportunity to rule the kingdom are all ways that characters have been given opportunities that made for great stories. *Notting Hill* features two characters who both get unexpected opportunities.

The Decision

When a character gets an opportunity, it usually isn't without consequence. Watching someone be forced to make a decision between two extremely compelling or less than compelling options is one way to develop that character and create plot around them. For example, in *Brooklyn*, Saoirse Ronan's character must choose between her life and family in Ireland and the new opportunities and relationships in America.

10 WRITING PROMPTS FOR DEVELOPING A NEW SCRIPT IDEA

In order to take advantage of these prompts, all you need is a character. Use one you've been developing recently. If you don't have one of your own, feel free to use one of these:

Katie Boleyn: Caucasian, mid 30s, lives in Washington, D.C. She works for a Congresswoman.

Billy Niles: African-American, late 70s, lives in San Francisco. He's played the trumpet at the KitKat Club for over 40 years.

Andrea Lopez: Latina, early 20s, lives in Dallas. She's gay and comes from a religious family.

Steve Simmons: Asian, late 20s, lives in Atlanta. He's a kindergarten teacher.

THE WORST DAY
Imagine the worst day in your character's life. Write for ten minutes about the day this event occurred. If the juices are flowing, write about the day *after* the event.

THE BIG SECRET
Imagine your character is hiding a secret that no one knows. Perhaps they accidentally killed someone. Perhaps they are in love with their boss. Perhaps they stole money from their church's collection plate. Who is the one person they *definitely* wouldn't want to find out about their secret? Write 2-3 pages about the secret and its discovery.

THE MYSTERIOUS STRANGER

Imagine a mysterious stranger suddenly appears in your character's life that seems to know things about them that no one else does. Write a single page about the moment the stranger appears and exactly what they know.

THE GHOST

Imagine someone from your character's past suddenly shows up. Their appearance is upsetting to your character. Write for five minutes about why your character never wanted to see this person again.

THE BIG RISK

Imagine your character decides to take the biggest risk of their life. What would that risk be? How would they go about executing it? Write for ten minutes about this.

THE RUNAWAY

Imagine your character must suddenly leave their life and run away. What caused this? What will they do? What are they leaving behind? What will they make an attempt to take with them? Write 2-3 pages about this.

THE WITNESS

Imagine your character witnesses something no one else was supposed to see. What will they do with this information? Did anyone see them witness the situation? Write for five minutes, describing everything that would go through your character's head.

THE DESCENDANT

Imagine your character is the son or daughter of someone famous. Do they embrace this fact or reject it? Does it help them in life or hurt them? Write a single page of biographical information about your character.

THE COLLECTOR

Imagine your character collects something very odd – something they would rather no one knew about. Write for ten minutes about what they collect, how they got into this hobby, and the implications of others knowing about it.

THE ABSURDIST

Imagine your character wakes up and finds a clown hiding in the corner of their room. Write 2-3 pages about the next ten minutes that occur.